Writing Skills, Grad[e]

Contents

Introduction 1
Scoring Rubric for Writing 4
Writing Conference Record 5
Diagnostic Sample Narratives 6
Sample How-to Papers 9
Sample Persuasive Papers 12
Proofreading Marks 16
The Writing Process 17
Types of Writing 18

Unit 1: Personal Narrative 20
Unit 2: Autobiographical Sketch 28
Unit 3: Descriptive Story 36
Unit 4: How-to Paper 44
Unit 5: Compare and Contrast Paper 52
Unit 6: Short Report 61
Unit 7: Persuasive Letter 69
Unit 8: Persuasive Movie Review 77
Unit 9: Persuasive Essay 85

Answer Key 93

Introduction

Language expression is an important skill for students to master. Learning to write helps students to interact with the larger world. It helps them to construct personal meaning and to communicate personal experiences. Writing well is the foundation for success in most school subjects.

One way to learn to write better is through imitation. *Writing Skills* gives students practice in reading and writing different types of papers. Students read original papers written by experienced writers, respond to what they read, analyze what they read, plan and organize writing ideas, write and revise drafts, and practice self-assessment. In addition, students have the opportunities to apply instructional standards, refresh their writing and language skills, build their confidence as writers, and prepare for standardized writing tests.

Standards for English Language Arts

The National Council of Teachers of English (NCTE) has stressed that "all students must have the opportunities and resources to develop the language skills they need to pursue life's goals and to participate fully as informed, productive members of society." The NCTE also states that students need to "apply a wide range of strategies as they write and use different writing process elements appropriately to communicate with different audiences for a variety of purposes." This book helps students to practice a variety of writing strategies. To learn more about the NCTE's twelve standards for the development of creative and innovative Language Arts curricula and instruction, visit **http://www.ncte.org/standards/**.

Organization

The book is divided into nine units. Each unit deals with a different type of writing. Each unit has seven parts. First, students read a Model Paper. Then, they Respond to the Model Paper. Next, they Analyze the Model Paper. After they have studied the model paper, they begin the process of writing their own paper. They receive a Writing Assignment, which includes a graphic organizer. A page is provided for the students to begin their First Draft. Once the first draft is complete, they begin to Revise the Draft. Then, they evaluate their own work or that of a classmate using a Writing Report Card.

Diagnostic Writing Prompt and Sample Papers

When you begin a writing program with your class, an informal assessment of students' writing skills helps you determine their initial strengths and weaknesses. Use the narrative prompt below to obtain diagnostic anchor papers for your class. Evaluate these papers using the Scoring Rubric on page 4. Before you begin the evaluation process, you may want to examine the sample papers and commentaries (pages 6–15). The papers are examples of student writing at each level of the rubric. The commentaries provide explanations of why each paper received its rating. All the sample papers are assigned a value from 4 to 1 using the Scoring Rubric on page 4.

Ask students to discuss or use their own paper to respond to the following questions:

1. What is the best thing that has ever happened to you?

2. When and where did it happen?

3. What made it so special?

Then, read the following directions aloud: *Write a story describing the best thing that ever happened to you. Give details that help your readers to imagine the story you tell.*

Encourage students to plan before writing their narrative. Suggest that they list the main ideas they will write about. Tell them to put the main ideas in the order they will write about them. Remind students to give details that support each main idea.

Proofreading Symbols

A chart of proofreading symbols is included on page 16. Students are encouraged to use these symbols as they edit and revise drafts. You may want to post the proofreading symbols as a ready reference for students.

Scoring Student Writing

Many states now include writing assessments in their statewide testing programs. The evaluation of these assessments often relies upon a state-specific scoring rubric. You may use your state's scoring rubric to evaluate your students' writing performance and progress. If your state does not provide a rubric, you may use the 4-point Scoring Rubric on page 4 that was used to evaluate the sample papers provided in this book. Still another option is the *6 + 1 Traits™ of Analytic Writing Assessment Scoring Guide*. This guide and sample student papers that have been evaluated using this guide can be found at **http://www.nwrel.org/assessment/**.

Writing Conference Record

A Writing Conference Record can be found on page 5. Questions and directions in the record help you evaluate each student's writing process skills and determine performance objectives. Records are used within the context of student-teacher conferences. Conferences promote dialogue about the writing experience and prompt discussion of ideas for writing, critical analysis, and opportunities for reading aloud. Conferences also help distinguish writing as a purposeful and rewarding activity.

Additional Writing Prompts

Additional writing prompts for each kind of writing are included below. These prompts can be used to give students additional writing practice in one or more kinds of writing. They can also be used as reinforcement in other instructional settings, in learning centers, and for homework. Encourage students to use writing plans to organize their thoughts and notes before writing a draft.

Personal Narrative

1. Think of something that makes you laugh. It may be a friend who shares your sense of humor, or it may be a pet that does unexpected things. Write a story describing a time when you couldn't stop laughing. Include details that help readers picture the events in your story.

2. Sometimes you can learn a lot about yourself when you are sick. Think of a time you were ill. Who took care of you? What kind of patient were you? How did you get over the illness? Write a story telling about this time in your life.

3. Think of something you do well. How did you learn this skill? When do you use it? Write a story describing your skill and how it makes your life more interesting.

4. Neighbors are an important part of our lives. Think of a neighbor that you will never forget. What makes this neighbor special? How did he or she affect your life? Write a story telling about this neighbor.

5. Some school activities are fun. Think about a recent activity at school that you enjoyed. What made it fun? Who was there? Why were you involved? Write a story describing this event.

Descriptive Story

1. Who is your favorite relative? Imagine that you get to spend a whole day with this person. Where will you go? What will you see and hear? Write a story using vivid, descriptive words that help your readers picture your experiences.

2. Look through children's books illustrated by well-known artists, such as Chris Van Allsburg or Denise Fleming. Choose one illustration that catches your attention. Use that illustration to brainstorm ideas for a descriptive story. Use at least two similes and two metaphors in your story.

3. Visit a busy location, such as a mall or the school cafeteria. Listen for interesting dialogue. Observe the scenes that you see. Make notes about the sights, sounds, and smells. Use your notes to write a story using this setting and some of the events you have witnessed. Use as many descriptive words as you can.

4. Do you have a favorite family holiday? Use that holiday as the subject of a descriptive story. Use words to describe what you see, hear, feel, taste, and smell.

5. Imagine that you are taking a family vacation to the best place on Earth. Write a descriptive story about your experience. Describe what you see, hear, feel, smell, and taste on your vacation.

How-to Paper

1. Think about a simple game, such as tic-tac-toe or checkers. Write a how-to paper describing how to play the game.

2. Have you ever made a collage or diorama to accompany a book report or science project? Make notes about the steps you took, from start to finish. Write a how-to paper describing how to create this type of art.

3. Think of a park or restaurant near your house. Make notes about the streets and turns that you use to get there. Then, write step-by-step directions for getting from your house to this location. As the final step, tell what you will do when you get there.

4. People take care of their teeth so they will stay healthy for a lifetime. Think about the steps in your daily dental-care routine. Then, write a how-to paper explaining this process.

5. Do you have a pet? What type of care does it need? Write a paper describing how to take care of your pet. Imagine that the directions are for a pet-sitter who will care for your pet while you are away on vacation.

Compare and Contrast Paper

1. Choose two people who are important in American history. When did they live? What contributions did they make? How did they affect our lives today? Gather information about these historical figures. Then, write a paper that explains their similarities and differences.

2. Have you read a book that has been made into a movie or cartoon? How are they alike? How are they different? Write a paper that compares and contrasts the two versions of the story.

3. Talk to an elderly relative or friend to learn what life was like when that person was your age. Use what you learn to write a compare and contrast paper about you and this person.

4. What do you most like to do when you are not in school? Think of two favorite activities. Then, write a paper that describes how they are alike and how they are different.

5. Many cultures around the world tell a version of the fairy tale about Cinderella. Use the library or the Internet to find two versions of the Cinderella story. Write a paper that compares and contrasts the two versions.

Short Report

1. People around the world celebrate special days. Choose a country and research its holidays. Then, write a short report.

2. There are many strange and wonderful plants in the world. Use reference materials to learn more about one plant. Then, write a short report.

3. Technology affects your life every day. Think about one item in your house that your parents didn't have when they were children. Use reference materials to learn more about this invention. Then, write a short report.

4. Products such as soft drinks and cereals often have a fascinating history. Choose one of your favorite products. Then, use reference materials to learn more about it. Write a short report to share what you learn.

5. Your community has a history all its own. Use reference materials, including local historians and newspapers, to learn more about the important events in your community's history. Then, share the information in a short report.

Persuasive Writing

1. Are you allowed to stay up as late as you think you should? What would you like your bedtime to be? Write a letter to convince your parents that you should be able to stay up later.

2. Parents and teachers at your school have asked the school board to stop selling sodas and candy in vending machines and in the cafeteria. They say students should eat more nutritious foods. What is your opinion? Write a persuasive essay for the school newspaper to convince others that your opinion is the right one.

3. Think about your favorite book. What makes it so special? Write a persuasive book review to convince all your friends to read the book.

4. A group of skateboarders has petitioned the city council to turn your neighborhood park into a skateboard park. What do you think about this idea? Write a persuasive essay expressing your opinion.

5. The local movie theater is considering a new rule that would require anyone under 14 to be accompanied by a parent, no matter what movie the person is seeing. Think about the reasons you are for or against this rule. Express your opinion in a persuasive letter to the owners of the movie theater.

Scoring Rubric for Writing

Score of 4
The student's response ...

- <u>clearly and completely</u> addresses the writing task,

- demonstrates an understanding of the purpose for writing,

- maintains a single focus,

- presents a central idea supported by relevant details and explanations,

- uses paragraphs to organize main ideas and supporting details under the umbrella of the central idea,

- presents content in a logical order or sequence,

- uses variety in sentence types and lengths,

- uses language appropriate to the writing task, such as language rich with sensory details in a model of descriptive writing,

- summarizes main ideas in a concluding paragraph in a model of expository or persuasive writing,

- establishes and defends a position in a model of persuasive writing, and

- has few or no errors in the standard rules of English grammar, punctuation, capitalization, and spelling.

Score of 3
The student's response ...

- <u>generally</u> follows the criteria described above, and

- has some errors in the standard rules of English grammar, punctuation, capitalization, and spelling, but not so many that a reader's comprehension is impaired.

Score of 2
The student's response ...

- <u>marginally</u> follows the criteria described above, and

- has several errors in the standard rules of English grammar, punctuation, capitalization, and spelling that may impair a reader's comprehension.

Score of 1
The student's response ...

- <u>fails</u> to follow the criteria described above, and

- has numerous and serious errors in the standard rules of English grammar, punctuation, capitalization, and spelling that impair a reader's comprehension.

Writing Conference Record

Encourage each student to share a writing sample with you. Then complete the conference record below. Invite each student to participate in several writing conferences. Use the records to assess each student's skills and progress.

Student's Name _____ Date _____

Title of the Writing Sample discussed today: _____

_____

Kind of writing this sample represents:

☐ Personal Narrative   ☐ How-to Paper   ☐ Persuasive Letter

☐ Narrative   ☐ Compare and Contrast Paper   ☐ Persuasive Movie Review

☐ Descriptive Story   ☐ Short Report   ☐ Persuasive Essay

Questions or Directions	Student's Responses and Teacher's Notes
What were your writing goals for this paper?	
Why did you choose this kind of writing?	
Why did you choose this topic?	
How did you organize your ideas and notes for this paper?	
Describe the writing process you used to write this paper, including revising your draft.	
What do you like most about this paper?	
In general, what is your strongest writing skill?	
Which writing skill do you think you need to improve? How will you do it?	

Date of next writing conference: _____

Diagnostic Sample Narratives

The following sample represents a narrative that meets the criteria for a 4-point paper.

Best Vacation Ever

We went down country roads and city streets. We passed through forests, lakes, mountains, valleys and canyons. We stopped at White Castles, which are a different kind of landmark. These are just some of the things my dad and I did when we left San Diego, California on a summer vacation. This turned out to be the best vacation ever.

Our first stop was Oshkosh, Wisconsin where we visited the largest airplane convention in the world. There were ultralights, amphibians, privates, commercials, some military planes, and even a few helicopters. What I saw most of were Cessna 182s. Those are privates, meaning they're owned by private owners. But what I thought was the most awesome airplane there was an amphibian ultralight. Now some of you are probably wondering what that is. Well, an amphibian is an airplane that can land on water and on land. An ultralight is like a hang-glider but with a motor, seat and steering.

The airplane convention was the first part of our vacation. Then we left Wisconsin and drove to Illinois to see my grandfather at his retirement home near Chicago. We stayed with my Aunt Nancy and Uncle David in Chicago. My uncle breeds German Shepherds and he had new puppies for sale. My dad and I stayed at my uncle's house for almost a week and during that time I fell in love with my puppy. He was fuzzy and his feet were too big for his body. He made me laugh every time I looked at him so I called him Chuckles.

My dad, Chuckles, and I went to Arkansas after that. My dad wanted to see what had happened to his land. He owned land there but he hadn't touched it in years. I have to give it credit for having lots of trees but I thought the land was really nasty. The ground was muddy and I've never seen so many flies.

That wasn't the best part of our trip, but we left there and went to a lake where my dog went swimming for the first time! The water there was more crystal clear than Lake Tahoe. The sun was shining off the water. My dad floated while I looked for rocks on the bottom of the lake. The weather was beautiful, and the water was the perfect temperature. Arkansas was our last stop. We drove straight home after we left. It was a long ride home, but it was worth it. Our summer vacation was the best thing that ever happened to me.

Commentary

The writer understood the purpose of this writing assignment and completed it with great success. He or she maintains a consistent focus, presents important events sequentially, and offers significant examples to support the paper's central premise. Numerous details help readers visualize the experience.

The writer organizes content chronologically and uses paragraphs to carry readers easily through the vacation experience. The organization of content and the strong introduction and conclusion are particular strengths of this paper. The explanation of the amphibian ultralight indicates the writer's awareness of his or her audience and his or her desire to communicate clearly.

The writer follows the conventions of the English language. Existing errors are few and do not interfere with a reader's comprehension. Content organization, sentence variety, and vivid details make the paper enjoyable to read and worthy of the highest score.

(Go on to the next page.)

The following sample represents a narrative that meets the criteria for a 3-point paper.

The Best Thing That Ever Happened to Me

The best thing that ever happened to me was when my mom took some friends and me to Sea World. The first thing that we did was ride the Steel Eel. The Steel Eel is a big roller coaster. The second thing that we did was ride the Great White. It is also a roller coaster, but it has no bottom.

Another thing that we did was ride the log ride witch had a very long line. Finally it was our turn. My friend was tired and did not want to get wet so he ducked under the seat the whole ride. Well, I thought the ride was pretty long. When we were going down my cheeks were going in my eyes, my face was turning red, and my hair, oh my hair was in pain. It felt like it was going to come out.

Another thing that my friend and I did was we went allllll the way to the top of the big, may I add very big, tower and body surfed all the way threw the twisting and winding, flipping, twirling, tubes. Finally when we got to the bottom of the ride, we did it again. But this time we did it with tubes. Then we went all the way back up and did it again. We went threw all of the twisting, winding twirling, flipping tubes. It was fun.

Then after that, we went to see this whale. We got to sit in the front zone, and it would always splash us with salt water. Then after a long day, we went to the car and dried off. Then we went to a restrant to eat some food. After that we went the hotel and went swimming.

When I was running on the sidewalk at the hotel to jump in the pool, I slipped and busted my head open on the edge of the pool. My mom ran over to see if I was ok. I was, but there was blood everywhere. The bleeding stopped and I didn't have to go to the hospital.

Finally we went to bed. The next morning we woke up and packed and left for home. I was tired but happy. Now you can see that going to Sea World was the best thing that ever happened to me.

Commentary

This paper responds to the writing assignment. The writer shows an understanding of the purpose of the writing task, that is, to describe the best thing that ever happened to him or her.

The writer states the topic of the paper in the first sentence. The writer then hastens to provide details to support the topic. The writer could have developed the introduction more fully before providing specific details surrounding the event.

The writer supplies relevant details, some of which are quite vivid. For example, the writer describes a ride that makes his or her hair hurt. The writer uses verbs, such as *twisting, winding, flipping,* and *twirling,* to describe motion through a set of tubes. Such vivid language enables the reader to visualize the writer's experience and is one of this paper's strongest features.

The writer organizes main ideas and supporting details into logical paragraphs that help the reader follow the sequence of events. However, the writer loses focus toward the end of the paper, describing an experience that occurred at the hotel. The conclusion is adequate, but like the introduction, could be improved.

The writer follows conventions of the English language. There are some errors in spelling, grammar, and punctuation, but they do not interfere with the reader's understanding.

(Go on to the next page.)

The following sample represents a narrative that meets the criteria for a 2-point paper.

The Best Day of My Life

The best thing that ever happened to me was when I went to Six Flags Fiesta Texas. I got to go in the summer of 1997 with my sister, my cousin, my uncle, my aunt, my mom, and my dad.

We went to the Six Flags in San Antonio. It was a big place and I'm glad I didn't get lost. My dad told me that if I got lost, to find a person who works there and ask them to help me. But that place was so big I don't think I could find one if I tried.

In conclusen, it was a special day because I got to ride a lot of rides, (my favorite one was none because it was to hard to pick,) and because I had a good time.

Commentary

The writer addresses part of the writing task in that he or she identifies the best thing that ever happened. However, the writer misunderstood the purpose of the task. While the writer identifies the visit to an amusement park as significant, he or she fails to elaborate. There are few main ideas, limited details, minimal recall of significant events, and no descriptive language. The writer fails to supply meaningful observations and memories.

The paper has some organization but lacks a clear beginning, middle, and end. Although the writer makes reference to a conclusion, in fact, there isn't one. Nor is there sufficient material in the body of the paper to make a conclusion necessary. There are errors in spelling, punctuation, and grammar. In themselves, they do not interfere with understanding. However, this paper's lack of development cannot be ignored as a major flaw, thus giving the paper a rating of two points.

The following sample represents a narrative that meets the criteria for a 1-point paper.

The best thing that ever happend was when my grandparents and I drove down to Floriada. It happened in about July. It occored first along the East coast, than the souther coast. It was special to me because I got to go throug different states like, new York, Conneticutt, Pennsylvania and so many, many more. It was even more special because I was with my gand parents.

Commentary

The writer identifies the topic of this paper in the first sentence but fails to address the task. Given that the writer assigned no title to the paper and that the paper's beginning, middle, and end occur together in the first paragraph, it is clear that the writer had little or no understanding of the purpose of this writing assignment.

The writer presents no sequence of events and fails to share a single observation or memory other than an approximation of when the event occurred. Descriptive language is absent, as are details that would enable the reader to imagine the experience. Problems in spelling affect the reader's ability to understand the paper's severely limited content. This writer's failure to address the writing task and the complete lack of development give the paper the minimum score of one point.

Sample How-to Papers

Before you begin the evaluation process, you may want to examine the following student papers and commentaries. The papers are examples of student writing at each level of the rubric. The commentaries provide explanations of why each paper received its rating.

The following sample represents a how-to paper that meets the criteria for a 4-point paper.

Shooting the Ring Variation

Shooting the Ring Variation is part of the game of marbles. There are just a few things you need to play. They include five marbles and a "shooter." A shooter is a marble larger than the average marble. You also need chalk and two to six players. The game requires a fair degree of skill and lasts about 10–20 minutes.

First, players select a reasonably flat surface and draw in chalk a circle about 2.5 m (8 ft.) in diameter. Each player then places one marble on the perimeter of the circle, making sure that the gaps between the marbles are roughly equal. A line is drawn about 1.8 m (6 ft.) from the edge of the ring. This line forms the shooting line.

Each person takes his shooter and rolls it into the center of the circle to determine the order of play. Whoever's closest to the center plays first. The next closest player is second, and so on.

The object of the game is to hit one of the marbles on the circle's edge with sufficient force that both the target marble and the shooter end up outside the circle. If this happens, the marble that was the target is captured and the player has another go. The shot is unsuccessful if the target marble is missed or the target is hit but stays inside the circle. Nevertheless, the player keeps the shooter.

The game ends when there are no more marbles left on the circle's rim. The winner is the person that has captured the most marbles. Have fun!

Commentary

The writer understands the writing task completely. He or she also remains focused throughout the paper. The paper has a clear beginning, middle, and end, and the writer follows the conventions of the English language.

The writer describes all of the necessary steps and important details to "shoot the ring variation." Consequently, a reader attempting this marble game could follow these directions and play successfully.

The writer's ability to describe steps thoroughly and organize information logically is exceptional. The paper is well developed and a good example of a 4-point paper.

(Go on to the next page.)

Sample How-to Papers, page 2

The following sample represents a how-to paper that meets the criteria for a 3-point paper.

How to Babysit: My Little Brother

Materials: 4 Rescue Heros movies, Rescue Heros action figures, 2 comfortable chairs, blanket & kitty, string cheese, pepsi, sprinkle popsicle bar, a phone, emergency phone #s

Warning: This mission is for professionals only. Please avoid if prone to motion sickness or have a delicate heart or eardrum! Helmet not included.

Steps:

1. Rush Nick upstairs and pop in a "Rescue Heros" movie.
2. Supply him with his blanket, kitty, string cheese, pepsi, and "Rescue Heros" action figures.
3. Sit down and play "Rescue Heros" with him. If he decides to play be himself or is preoccupied by the movie (hopefully!), feel free to relax.
4. Repeat steps 1, 2, and 3 until the movies are finished or he begins to get restless. Then, praise him for being so good, give him a sprinkle popsicle and bathe him.
5. Dress him nicely and comb his hair (If this step will not work, just get him dressed in anything!)
6. Now, have him sit next to you in one of the chairs and read him a story until parents return.
7. Summarize Nick's behavior for the parents and then get paid and get the hec-out-out-of-dodge! (unless you live there like me!)

Note: Try to keep Nick calm during your time babysitting him. If he is hyper though and you can't get him to listen to you, get red lipstic, put it on heavily and smooch him until he promises to listen. It works every time!

Commentary

The writer understood the purpose of this writing task and offers an amusing description of how to care for his or her little brother. The focus of the paper is never declared other than in the title. The writer does, however, list the necessary materials and the steps in the babysitting process in the order they should be followed.

The writer uses a clever warning to engage readers and then uses humor to keep their interest. Humor also leads the reader to infer that babysitting Nick is a difficult task. The writer maintains a consistent focus and provides specific, albeit unelaborated, details.

Given the writer's charming sense of humor, an introduction, conclusion, and more development of details could have elevated this paper's rating. The errors in the conventions of the English language do not interfere with comprehension; however, they suggest the writer's lack of attention to detail.

(Go on to the next page.)

© Steck-Vaughn Company

The following sample represents a how-to paper that meets the criteria for a 2-point paper.

How to Ice Skate

Have you ever ice skated? Do you even know how? Well I'm going to tell you how to skate and have fun.

First, you have to get skates. You can either get your own or use the ones you can rent from the ice arena. Then, you have to get to the ice arena. You can have a friend, parent, or yourself take you there. If a friend takes you, get him or her to come too. Now, when you put on your skates, you need to make sure you tie them tight. You tie them kind of like you tie your shoes. You have to make sure there tight or you can hurt yourself. Finally, (if you have long hair) you can put your hair back with a hair tie, so your hair doesn't get in you face. And get your balance. Lastly, grab your friend, head out on the ice and have fun.

Commentary

The writer sets out to teach someone to ice skate, a task too large to explain in a how-to paper. In this case, the writer assumes that putting on skates makes the wearer an ice skater. Clearly, steps are missing.

The writer presents a central idea but stops short of his or her goal. The sequence of events takes the reader to the beginning, not the end, of the ice-skating process. Details are inadequate and organized poorly. There are some errors in the conventions of the English language; however, these mistakes do not interfere with a reader's understanding.

The following sample represents a how-to paper that meets the criteria for a 1-point paper.

I know how to do math really well. The materials you need to do math are a sharpened pencil, a sheet of paper, and a calculator. The steps you should do is go from easiest to hardest. For example, learn adition first, subtaction next, then, multiplycation, and divide last. The steps to do a problem are first, write down a problem, second, you should work the problem from right to left and for division left to right. Third, look at the answer and check it on a calculator, last, you are done with the problem.

Commentary

The writer attempts to teach a reader how to do something. That was the essence of the writing task. However, it is clear that the writer does not understand the fundamental challenges of a how-to paper. Those challenges include choosing a specific topic, identifying the materials and skills necessary to do the task, and explaining the specific steps in the process so that a reader can complete the task successfully.

The paper includes no topic sentence identifying what the writer intends to teach the reader. The writer lists materials; however, materials alone do not guarantee success in math. The writer offers few details to guide the reader. Existing details are vague and unhelpful. Errors in spelling, grammar, and punctuation interfere with comprehension.

Sample Persuasive Papers

Before you begin the evaluation process, you may want to examine the following student papers and commentaries. The papers are examples of student writing at each level of the rubric. The commentaries provide explanations of why each paper received its rating.

The following sample represents a persuasive movie review that meets the criteria for a 4-point paper.

"Indiana Jones and the Last Crusade"

Hello movie fans! I want to tell you about one of the classics. "Indiana Jones and the Last Crusade" is an exciting movie that you enjoy every time you see it. Harrison Ford is his usual 5-star self as he mixes action with humor.

This exciting movie has traps that grab your mind and throw you into suspense. It has creepy effects and the traps seem impossible to escape, but Indiana Jones escapes them all. Jones and his father have a quest. They must find the Holy Grail, the cup used at the Last Supper, before the Nazis do. The cup has divine healing powers. It also has the power to destroy.

This movie is as funny as it is suspenseful. During their trek across the desert, Jones and his father encounter the Nazis. Harry Jones, Indiana Jones' father, gets captured. He squirts pen in his abductor's face to let him go. The pen is stronger than the sword!

The story is painted with suspense. In the beginning, young Indiana tries to get the Cross of Coronado but fails. During the chase, he falls into a pit of snakes and even faces a lion!

This story is a movie for the great adventurer. Every time you see it, you scream, you laugh, and you have a good time!

Commentary

The writer's enthusiasm may be enough to convince readers who love adventure movies to see this "classic." The writer presents the movie as a story that combines "action with humor." Then the writer offers specific examples to support the claim.

The writer's focus is consistent, the content is organized logically, and the details are specific and interesting. The paper has a clear beginning, middle, and end. The writer prioritizes reasons to see the film and uses the conclusion to entice readers a last time. The writer follows conventions of the English language and uses a variety of sentence types. One of the best features of the paper is the writer's style. The writer uses a consistent and energetic personal voice that makes the paper a pleasure to read.

(Go on to the next page.)

The following sample represents a persuasive movie review that meets the criteria for a 3-point paper.

The Others

The best movie I have seen is "The Others." If you like your movies to be scary you should see this one. This movie is horrifying. It also has special effects that will knock your socks off.

The movie is about a woman who seems crazy. She has two kids and they live together in a haunted house. Other people live there too. They are servants who take care of the house and the garden. The servants know a secret that they don't tell the woman and her kids.

The husband comes back for a little while. Then he goes away again. You find out why later. You also find out about the Others.

I love scary movies and this is the best one I've seen. The movie is full of suspense. But there's no blood. I kept my eyes open through the whole thing. If you like scary movies, see "The Others." You'll be scared to death.

Commentary

The writer sets out to convince readers to see a frightening movie and to some degree, succeeds. The writer generally maintains a consistent focus and attempts to organize content in a logical way. There is a central idea supported with some details, and events are presented in an appropriate sequence. The writer follows most conventions of the English language.

The paper has two general weaknesses. The first is its failure to elaborate upon the movie's special effects. While the writer's decision to introduce this feature in the first paragraph may have been a good idea, it fell short of its goal when the writer offered no further discussion. The absence of elaboration in this example is indicative of the paper's second general weakness. Overall, more specific details could have improved this paper and made the paper more persuasive.

(Go on to the next page.)

The following sample represents a persuasive movie review that meets the criteria for a 2-point paper.

> On October 2, The Mummy Returns came out on VHS and DVD. I thought it was very good. It stars Brendan Fraser and Rachel Weisz. The Rock is the Scorpion King. It has been rated PG-13.
>
> The movie takes place nine years after the first movie. Rick O'Connell and Evelyn, the main characters, have gotten married and have an 8 year old boy named Alex. Alex puts the bracelet of Anubis on and 7 days to find the Scorpion King's resting place. Things can't get any worse. Wrong! Imhatep has been brought back to life by Anck-Su-Namum! It's up to Rick to help Alex. Can they do it? Go find out.

Commentary

This paper reflects a limited understanding of the purpose of this writing assignment. The writer fails to state his or her position clearly. He or she also fails to support any implied position with relevant details.

The writer attempts to organize information into paragraphs. The first paragraph is dedicated to identifying the movie and its stars. In the second paragraph, the writer introduces the movie's plot. This is the first step in convincing readers to see the movie. However, the introduction is incomplete. The writer's descriptions are inadequate and leave readers with limited understanding of the movie's plot. More importantly, the writer fails to explain what makes this movie special. Even readers who love adventure films are left to wonder why they should see this movie.

There are few errors in the conventions of the English language and certainly none that inhibits a reader's comprehension. The dilemma is that the writer offers too little content for the reader to make an informed decision.

(Go on to the next page.)

The following sample represents a persuasive movie review that meets the criteria for a 1-point paper.

> Haven't seen a good movie in a while? Then you have to go see "Hardball." It is so funny because the actors in this movie are mainly children and you know how funny children can be sometimes! If you enjoy occasionally crying at movies, then this is the movie for you. See "Hardball" today and enjoy!!!!!!

Commentary

The first two sentences suggest that the writer understands the purpose of this writing task and is prepared to address its parts. However, that is not the case. The writer has little to say about the movie. Existing details are inadequate and contradictory.

Contrary to most 1-point papers, this paper does not have errors in the conventions of the English language that will interfere with a reader's comprehension. However, it lacks a clear focus, has an unsupported central idea, lacks relevant details and explanations, and fails to satisfy the purpose for writing. The writer leaves a reader knowing nothing about the film except its title and that its actors are mainly children.

Proofreading Marks

Mark	Meaning	Example
◯	spell correctly	I (liek) dogs.
⊙	add period	They are my favorite kind of pet⊙
?	add question mark	Are you lucky enough to have a dog?
≡	capitalize	My dog's name is scooter.
℘	take out	He is a great companion for me and my ~~my~~ family.
∧	add	We got Scooter when ^he^ was eight weeks old.
/	make lower case	My /Uncle came over to take a look at him.
∽	trade places	He watched the puppy run ⌐in⌐around⌐ circles.
،	add comma	"Jack، that dog is a real scooter!" he told me.
∨ ∨	add quotation marks	⌄Scooter! That's the perfect name!⌄ I said.
¶	indent paragraph	¶ Scooter is my best friend in the whole world. He is not only happy and loving but also the smartest dog in the world. Every morning at six o'clock, he jumps on my bed and wakes me with a bark. Then he brings me my toothbrush.

The Writing Process

In writing, you can use a plan to help you think of ideas and then write about them. This plan is called a *writing process*. Here are the steps of the writing process.

Step 1: Prewriting

Think about why you are writing. What is your purpose, or goal? Who are you writing for?

Choose a topic, or something to write about. Make notes. Organize your notes in a way that makes sense.

Step 2: Drafting

Use your ideas and notes from the first step to begin writing.

Step 3: Revising

Read your draft. Is the purpose of your paper clear?

Share your writing with someone else. Talk about what is good about your paper and what could make it better.

Step 4: Proofreading

Correct any mistakes you find in spelling, grammar, punctuation, and capitalization.

Step 5: Publishing

Make a clean copy of your paper.

Share your paper with others.

Moving Back and Forth

All together, there are five steps in the writing process. However, as you write, you may move back and forth through the steps several times before you reach your writing goal.

You may return to your draft many times to make it better. Go back and forth often. The extra steps will improve your writing and help you publish your best work.

Types of Writing

In this book you will read examples of different kinds of writing. Then you will practice your own writing skills. You will write to…

- **Tell a Story**
  A story is also called a narrative. A narrative has…
  - one or more characters.
  - a setting, or place and time for the story to happen.
  - a plot that includes a problem that is solved step by step.

- **Tell About a Part of Your Life**
  An autobiographical sketch tells about part of your life. It includes…
  - important events that happened to you.
  - details that describe the events that happened.

- **Describe Someone or Something**
  When you describe something or someone, you share details. Details can be…
  - facts.
  - information that comes from using your senses of hearing, sight, smell, touch, and taste.
  - dialogue, or words that people say.
  - thoughts and feelings.

- **Explain How to Do Something**
  When you explain how to do something, you talk about…
  - the materials someone needs.
  - the steps someone should follow in order.
  - important details.

- **Show How Two Things, Places, or People Are Alike and Different**
  To explain how two things are alike and different, you…
  - use reference materials to find information on a topic.
  - organize main ideas about the topic to show how two things are alike.
  - organize main ideas about the topic to show how two things are different.
  - include important details.

Types of Writing, page 2

- **Share Information in a Short Report**
  To write a good report, you…
  - choose a specific topic.
  - decide what you would like to learn about your topic.
  - use reference materials to collect information about your topic.
  - use facts, not opinions.

- **Convince Someone**
  When you write persuasively, you…
  - share your opinion or position on a topic.
  - try to make someone agree with you.
  - try to convince someone to do something.

A Model Paper

A Personal Narrative

The Yearbook Contest

On my first day in my new school, I pretty much stayed to myself. No one talked to me, and I didn't talk to them. By fifth period, I was tired and ready to go home. Then something wonderful happened. A girl in the second row smiled at me. I'll never forget that smile.

Maria helped me start a new life. From the very beginning, she was special. We shared everything, even our secrets. She tutored me when I got a "C" in math, and I cheered her up when a boy she liked asked someone else to the Autumn Dance. Maria and I talked on the phone for hours, painted each other's toenails, and did our homework together. We were like sisters.

Maria was so important to me that I thought we'd be friends forever. Nothing could come between us. Until the yearbook contest, that is.

The yearbook staff advertised a school-wide contest. They were looking for a design for the yearbook cover. The theme of the book was "togetherness." About two seconds after I read the announcement, I entered the contest. I figured a seventh or eighth grader would probably win, but I was going to enter anyway. Drawing was my favorite hobby, and I was good at it. Everybody said so, even Maria.

I spent the next couple of weeks coming up with a perfect design. I didn't tell anyone, not even Maria. I wanted to wait until it was finished. Then I'd show it to her.

The deadline arrived and I took my design to school. I couldn't wait to show the design to Maria before I turned it in, but I couldn't find her. I left my design at the yearbook office and then went to class.

I finally found Maria at lunch. I gabbed on and on about my design and the contest, thinking Maria might say something about it, but she didn't. When lunch was over, Maria said with a voice sadder than I'd ever heard her use before, "That's great, Jessica. Good luck." She turned and left me standing in the hallway. I was shocked. Something was very wrong.

I didn't see Maria for the rest of the day. As soon as I got home from school, I called her. At first she wouldn't tell me what was wrong. So I kept asking. Finally, she admitted that she had entered the contest, too. My heart sank. How could we both be in the same contest? I didn't know what to say. Then she explained that her brother had convinced her to enter. "I'm sorry," Maria said. "I'm going to take my design back. Our friendship means more to me than a contest."

"No, Maria, it's okay. I'm just surprised, that's all. You never talk about the art class you take. And you never said anything about entering the contest," I said.

"Jessica, you never told me you were going to enter either," she said. "Anyway, I don't have a chance of winning."

"Gosh, Maria, you're right. I don't mean about not having a chance of winning. I mean about me. I was upset because you didn't tell me you entered the contest, but I didn't tell you either. I'm sorry. You know, I've never seen any of your art. I bet you're great."

"Well, not great, but I have a few things I like. Would you like to see them?" she asked.

I put down the phone and raced to Maria's house. She reached under her bed and pulled out a huge folder with leather straps. "Wow. That's a cool folder," I said. "Where'd you get it?"

"My brother made it for me. He loves my work. He tells me I'm going to be a famous artist one day." Maria showed me her work. Maria's brother was right. Maria's work was fantastic. I couldn't let her back out of the contest for me. That afternoon we made a deal. We would both leave our work in the contest and still be best friends, no matter who won. We did, and we are. Maria gave me her winning design as a birthday present that year. I still have it.

Respond to the Model Paper

Directions ▷ Write your answers to the following questions or directions.

1. The theme of the yearbook contest was "togetherness." What is the theme of this story?

   _____

   _____

2. What are some of the ways the writer lets you know how she felt about Maria?

   _____

   _____

   _____

   _____

3. Write a paragraph to summarize the story. To help you write, think about the main ideas in the story. Also think about how the story ends.

   _____

   _____

   _____

   _____

   _____

   _____

   _____

   _____

   _____

   _____

Analyze the Model Paper

 **Directions** ⟩ Read "The Yearbook Contest" again. As you read, think about how the writer wrote the story. Write your answers to the following questions.

1. How do you know that this is a personal narrative?

   _____

   _____

   _____

   _____

2. Read the third paragraph again. What does the writer present in this paragraph?

   _____

   _____

   _____

   _____

3. Read the last paragraph again. How do the characters solve the problem in this story?

   _____

   _____

   _____

   _____

4. How does the writer let you know who won the contest without telling you directly?

   _____

   _____

   _____

   _____

Writing Assignment

 **Directions** ➤ Think about someone you know who is special to you. Write a personal narrative about this person. Use examples and details to show why this person is special. Use this writing plan to help you write.

Writing Plan

Who is the person you will write about?

Tell what makes this person special to you.

Give examples to show why this person is special.

First Draft

Tips for Writing a Personal Narrative:

- Write from your point of view. Use the words I and my to show your readers that this is your story.
- Think about what you want to tell your reader.
- Organize your ideas into a beginning, middle, and end.
- Write an interesting introduction that "grabs" your readers.
- Write an ending for your story. Write it from your point of view.

First Draft

Directions Use your writing plan as a guide for writing your first draft of a *Personal Narrative*.

_____

_____

_____

_____

_____

_____

_____

_____

_____

_____

_____

_____

(Continue on your own paper.)

Name _____ Date _____

Revise the Draft

Directions ⟩ Use the chart below to help you revise your draft. Check *Yes* or *No* to answer each question in the chart. If you answer *No*, make notes to remind yourself how you can revise, or change, your writing to improve it.

Question	Yes ✔	No ✔	If the answer is no, what will you do to improve your writing?
Does your story describe someone special to you?			
Do you use specific examples to explain why this person is special?			
Does your story have a strong beginning?			
Do you describe events in the order they happened?			
Does your story have a strong ending?			
Do you use different kinds of sentences, such as questions and dialogue, to make your story interesting?			
Do you tell your story from your point of view?			
Have you corrected mistakes in spelling, grammar, and punctuation?			

Directions ⟩ Use the notes in your chart and writing plan to revise your draft.

Name _____ Date _____

Writing Report Card

 **Directions** > Read your revised draft again or ask someone else to read it. Have the person who reads your paper complete the following Report Card. Revise your paper until you have no less than a Very Good Score for each item.

Title of paper: _____

Purpose of paper: _____**This paper is a personal narrative. It talks about**_____

_____**someone who is special to me.**_____

Person who scores the paper: _____

Score	Writing Goals
	Does the writer tell this story from a personal point of view?
	Does the story have a strong beginning?
	Does the story include specific examples to explain why the person in the story is special?
	Are there details to support each example?
	Are the paragraphs organized in a way that makes sense?
	Are there different kinds of sentences, such as questions and dialogue, that help make the story interesting?
	Does the story have a strong ending?
	Are the story's grammar, spelling, and punctuation correct?

☺ Excellent Score   ☆ Very Good Score   + Good Score

✔ Acceptable Score   — Needs Improvement

A Model Paper

An Autobiographical Sketch

July the Fourth on the Llano River

We have family reunions every July 4th. I can't remember any of them but one. It was last year when we met at the Llano River. That's when I learned to swim.

We arrived at my aunt's house on Friday night. My cousin J.W. was already there. J.W. is in high school. He is loud and funny, and a real pain. Every summer, he finds one of us younger kids and picks on us the whole time we are together. That year, it was my turn.

It started as soon as he saw me. "Hey, kid," he asked, "did you ever learn to swim? Are you going to do that doggy paddle thing again this year?" I hung my head down, embarrassed in front of my other cousins. My embarrassment didn't seem to bother J.W. He kept right on poking fun. "You know, kid, you remind me a lot of Aunt Betty's cocker spaniel when you're in the water. Pant, splash, pant, splash. Don't get me wrong. I love it. It's a scream, and probably makes you popular with all of your friends back home. That's how everyone swims there, right?" I slipped away as quietly as I could.

The next morning, all the kids went down to the river right after breakfast. I sat around with the grown-ups. I couldn't bring myself to go down to the river. I kept talking to myself, building up my courage. It took until lunchtime for me to find it.

I grabbed a towel from the bathroom closet, put on my flip-flops, and marched down to the river. I may look like a cocker spaniel, but who cared? It was just J.W. talking, and his opinion, I didn't need. Most of my cousins were in the water, splashing, tubing, and diving for pennies.

The afternoon sun was warm and made the water feel great. I dragged one of the inner tubes on the bank into the water and plopped inside it. I wasn't afraid to float down the rapids in a tube. It was fun, and I stayed on the surface of the water, even when the rapids were fast.

As I floated near the rapids, I saw my cousin Danny. He's a little guy and always funny to watch. He was too small for the tube and sat low. When the water shot him across the rocks, Danny bumped all the way down the river. He always got out at the end of the rapids rubbing his backside. He didn't seem to mind, though. Danny was always the first one to run back up the riverbank to get ahead of the rapids and start again.

Just below the rapids, the river had carved a deep swimming hole. I pulled my tube out of the water and watched my cousins playing from the bank. I really wanted to be out there with them, but what was the point? There was J.W., splashing, laughing, and dunking the little kids under the water. No way was I going out there.

About the time I was getting ready to leave, Donnie, my brother, swam over to the bank. He sat with me in a shallow place near some large rocks. The water was really warm there. We talked about the river, about swimming, and about J.W. Then Donnie did something surprising. He leaned over and whispered in my ear, "If you want to learn to swim, I'll help you." The idea sounded great to me. "Can you teach me now?" I asked excitedly. I remember that made Donnie laugh. "Hold on there, little spaniel, let's get in deeper water first," he said as he smiled.

We walked over to an area that was not too deep. Donnie showed me how to hold my face in the water and turn it to the side to breathe. I wasn't crazy about putting my face in the water at first. I had to practice for a while, but Donnie didn't seem to mind.

Next, he showed me how to move my arms in a big circle. Then we put breathing and circling together. When I could do both things at the same time, I thought I was ready. I didn't know what was coming next.

We moved into deeper water. I could still feel the river bottom squishing between my toes. Donnie told me to float on my back. That was easy. Then he told me to turn over and float on my stomach. That was hard. All of a sudden, water rushed into my nose. I couldn't breathe and I panicked. I started imitating a cocker spaniel again, a frightened one. So Donnie pulled my head up and helped me stand. I couldn't stop coughing and spitting out water. I think I spit out a tadpole, but Donnie told me I was imagining things.

When I looked up along the bank, I saw my mom and dad watching me. At first, my mom looked worried, but then I saw her smile. Her smile made me determined. I told Donnie I was ready to try again. We stayed in the water so long that my fingers shriveled like old raisins. At first, I swam circles around Donnie. Then the circles got bigger and bigger. I knew how to swim!

When I was too tired to move anymore, I swam back to where Donnie sat on the bank. By the time I got there, all of my cousins were there, too. Even J.W. was there. He helped me out of the water, slapped me on the back, and said, "Hey, little spaniel, you're not a puppy anymore." That was J.W.'s idea of a compliment, and I was glad to take it.

Respond to the Model Paper

Directions ▷ Write your answers to the following questions or directions.

1. In an autobiographical sketch, a writer talks about something important that happened to him or her. What important thing happened to this writer?

   _____

   _____

2. How would you describe the setting for this story?

   _____

   _____

3. What is the first clue the writer gives you to tell you what J.W. is like?

   _____

   _____

4. Based on the story, how would you describe the relationship between the writer and Donnie, her brother?

   _____

   _____

5. Write a paragraph to summarize the story. Think about the story's main ideas and what happens first, second, and so on. Also think about how the story ends.

   _____

   _____

   _____

   _____

   _____

   _____

Analyze the Model Paper

 **Directions** ⟩ Read "July the Fourth on the Llano River" again. As you read, think about how the writer wrote the story. Answer the following questions or directions.

1. How does the writer add emotion, or strong feeling, to this story?

   _____

   _____

   _____

   _____

2. Read the third paragraph again. Why do you think the writer used dialogue in this paragraph?

   _____

   _____

   _____

   _____

3. How does the writer use humor to tell this story?

   _____

   _____

   _____

   _____

4. What does the writer do to help you "see" J.W. as she sees him?

   _____

   _____

   _____

   _____

Writing Assignment

 **Directions** ⟩ Write an autobiographical sketch about something important that happened to you. Write about something you remember well. Use this writing plan to help you write.

Writing Plan

What important thing happened to you?

What happened first? How will you describe it?

What happened second? How will you describe it?

What happened last? How will you describe it?

First Draft

Tips for Writing an Autobiographical Sketch:

- Write about something important that happened to you.
- Write about something you remember well.
- Give details that help explain your experience.
- Describe events in the order that they happened.

First Draft

Directions ➤ Use your writing plan as a guide for writing your first draft of an *Autobiographical Sketch.*

_____

_____

_____

_____

_____

_____

_____

_____

_____

_____

(Continue on your own paper.)

Name _____   Date _____

Revise the Draft

Directions ⟩ Use the chart below to help you revise your draft. Check *Yes* or *No* to answer each question in the chart. If you answer *No*, make notes to remind yourself how you can revise, or change, your writing to improve it.

Question	Yes ✔	No ✔	If the answer is no, what will you do to improve your writing?
Does your autobiographical sketch describe something important that happened to you?			
Does your story have a clear setting?			
Do you include important characters in your story?			
Do you use specific details to help you tell your story?			
Do you describe events in the order they happened?			
Have you corrected mistakes in spelling, grammar, and punctuation?			

Directions ⟩ Use the notes in your chart and writing plan to revise your draft.

Name _____ Date _____

Writing Report Card

Directions ➤ Read your revised draft again or ask someone else to read it. Have the person who reads your paper complete the following Report Card. Revise your paper until you have no less than a Very Good Score for each item.

Title of paper: _____

Purpose of paper: _____ **This paper is an autobiographical sketch. It describes**

_____ **something important that happened in my life.**

Person who scores the paper: _____

Score	Writing Goals
	Is this story an example of an autobiographical sketch?
	Is the setting described in detail?
	Does the writer use important characters to help tell the story?
	Does the writer describe specific events?
	Does the writer use important details to help explain events?
	Does the writer describe events in the order they happen?
	Does the writer convince you that this experience was important to him or her?
	Are the story's grammar, spelling, and punctuation correct?

☺ Excellent Score   ☆ Very Good Score   + Good Score

✔ Acceptable Score   — Needs Improvement

Name _____ Date _____

A Model Paper

A Descriptive Story

Weekend Friends

Cole's dad was unusually late picking him up on Friday night. He didn't say anything to his mother, but Cole was a little worried. His dad was never late. Cole sat quietly, tracing the stitching in his overnight bag. Finally, the phone rang. Cole's mom rushed to the kitchen to answer it. "He's on his way," she announced with relief. "He got tied up at the office."

Soon Cole and his dad were in the car driving to his dad's apartment. "Sorry about that, Cole," his dad said. "Something came up at the office. I know it's too late to do much tonight. But," he added, "I have a special day planned tomorrow. I hope you don't mind."

"It's okay, Dad," Cole said quickly. Cole knew that their weekends together were as important to his dad as they were to him.

The next morning, golden rays spilled through Cole's bedroom window. Saturday had come. By the time his dad got up, Cole was already dressed and eating breakfast. "Wow," his dad said. "You're in a hurry this morning." His dad smiled. "Let me finish this cup of coffee, and we'll be on our way, okay?" Cole nodded.

The highway was a gray stripe through green countryside. On either side, wildflowers bounced in the wind. Their red and yellow heads moved up and down like fishing bobs on a lake. Cole's dad slowed the car and turned right onto a farm road. Then he turned again, this time onto a dirt road that sliced the pasture.

Cole's dad stopped the car. "Well, what do you think?" Cole looked puzzled. "What do you mean?" he asked.

His dad laughed softly. "This is our farm. This is why I was late last night. I had to sign the papers." Cole looked amazed. His eyes widened and his mouth fell open, but he couldn't speak a word.

Cole and his dad walked through the pasture to a row of graceful trees. The deep green live oaks and giant cottonwoods bowed over a narrow creek. The creek babbled like a child. The sun's rays sparkled on the water. Cole and his dad sat on the bank. "What do you think, Cole?" Cole turned slowly, forcing his eyes away from the creek. "I love it," he almost whispered.

Cole's dad took him towards the old farmhouse beyond the creek. "I thought we could come here on the weekends, Cole. We could fix up the house together. I could use the help. Wait until you see it. It's been empty for more than forty years."

"Who lived here then, Dad?" Cole asked. "I don't know," said his dad. "The agent said the last owner never used the house. He just let it fall down. He's the person who sold the farm." They reached the farmhouse and for the second time in one day, Cole didn't know what to say. This was the tallest, oldest, most run-down house he'd ever seen. He loved it.

"Wow!" Cole yelled. "Cool house! This is great!" Cole started running. His dad yelled, "Cole, slow down. You can't trust those steps. Wait." But Cole couldn't hear the last warning. It came just as Cole's leg went through a rotten step. The bottom half of his body disappeared, swallowed by the steps. Cole's dad raced toward him. "Are you okay, Cole? Can you move?" he asked, with panic in his voice.

Cole groaned a little as his dad pulled him from the step. "I'm fine, really. I don't think anything's broken." While his dad checked his legs, Cole lay on the porch. His head turned toward the jagged hole. "Dad, I think there's something in there. Look." Cole's dad ignored him as he continued to ask what hurt. "Dad, what is it?" Cole said. He'd forgotten about his legs. Cole's dad looked inside the hole. "I don't know, Cole, but you stay here. I'll go in this time." He squeezed through the hole, landing with a thud. When he came back up, he had a box caked in decades of dirt. He and Cole used a pocketknife to remove the dirt and pick the small, rusting lock that kept the box sealed.

"Wow," Cole and his dad said at the same time. Inside were a small leather box and a dirty envelope. Inside the box was a World War II Medal of Honor. Even now, the eagle shined and the ribbon looked fresh. Inside the envelope was a certificate and a single photograph. "Horace Mickel," Cole's dad said as he read the name on the certificate. "I'd say this medal and this house must have belonged to him."

"Who was Horace Mickel, Dad? Do you think he left anything else under those steps?" Cole asked. "Or in the house?" he added eagerly.

"I don't know," Cole's dad chuckled. "Let's forget the steps for now. If you think you can get yourself up, we'll start looking for the answers to your questions inside." Cole's dad unlocked the front door. He held Cole's elbow as Cole hobbled inside. The wind came with them, disturbing dust that had sat comfortably for forty years. Spider webs as fine as lace capped their heads. "This is great, Dad. It looks like Mr. Mickel left everything behind. There are bound to be clues everywhere."

"I think you're right, Cole. But I have an idea. Let's not try to find all of our answers today. Let's make this last awhile. Let's make this our weekend project, and we'll come to know Mr. Mickel a little at a time, just like friends normally do." Cole's dad hugged him hard.

"Good idea, Dad. I think I'll put this photograph above the fireplace. Then we'll know where to find Mr. Mickel when we come back."

Respond to the Model Paper

Directions ▷ Write your answers to the following questions or directions.

1. What makes this story an example of descriptive writing?

   _____

   _____

2. How does the writer let you know that Cole and his mom are nervous?

   _____

   _____

3. How does the writer let you know that Cole loves his dad, the farm, and the farmhouse?

   _____

   _____

4. Use a separate piece of paper to draw a picture of your favorite description in this story. Label your picture.

5. Write a paragraph to summarize the story. Use these questions to help you write your summary:

   • What are the main ideas of the story?
   • What happens first? Second? Third?
   • How does the story end?

   _____

   _____

   _____

   _____

   _____

   _____

Analyze the Model Paper

 **Directions** ⟩ Read "Weekend Friends" again. As you read, think about how the writer achieved his or her purpose for writing. Write your answers to the following questions or directions.

1. Read the fifth and eighth paragraphs again. What similes does the writer use? (A simile uses the word *like* or *as* to compare two things.)

     _____

     _____

2. What metaphor does the writer use in the fifth paragraph? (A metaphor does not use the word *like* or *as* to compare two things.)

     _____

     _____

3. List some interesting verbs the writer uses to describe the action in paragraphs 5, 8, 11, and 12.

     _____

     _____

4. Use a separate piece of paper to draw a picture of the description in paragraph 15.

5. Write a paragraph to describe what the farmhouse will look like when Cole and his dad finish fixing it up.

     _____

     _____

     _____

     _____

     _____

     _____

Name _____   Date _____

Writing Assignment

To describe something, a writer tells what he or she sees, hears, feels, tastes, and smells. The writer uses interesting words. The writer also compares things to other things, like a creek to a babbling child. Describe something that you and a relative or friend did together. Use this writing plan to help you write.

Writing Plan

 **Directions** → What experience would you like to describe? Write it in the circle. Then write words, similes, or metaphors that describe the experience on the lines.

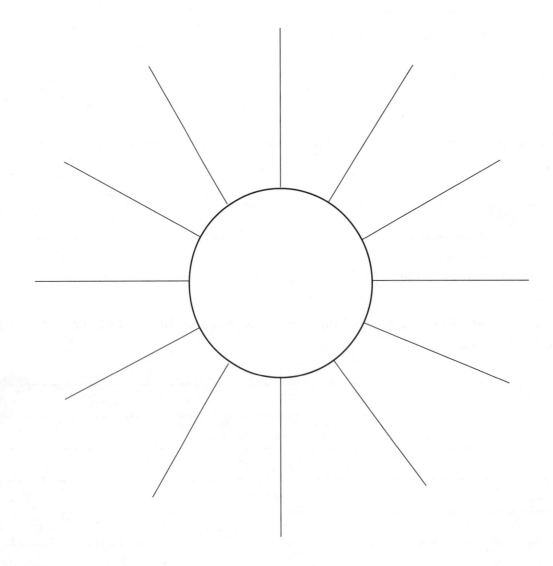

First Draft

Tips for Writing a Descriptive Story:

- Use your voice when you write. That means you should use your special way of expressing yourself.

- Help readers see, smell, taste, feel, and hear what you are writing about.

- Use interesting words to help you describe.

- Use similes and metaphors to help your readers imagine the experience you are writing about.

First Draft

Directions Use your writing plan as a guide as you write your first draft of a *Descriptive Story*.

_____

_____

_____

_____

_____

_____

_____

_____

_____

_____

(Continue on your own paper.)

Revise the Draft

Directions > Use the chart below to help you revise your draft. Check *Yes* or *No* to answer each question in the chart. If you answer *No*, make notes to remind yourself how you can revise, or change, your writing to improve it.

Question	Yes ✔	No ✔	If the answer is no, what will you do to improve your writing?
Do you describe something that happened to you and a relative or friend?			
Do you describe what you see, hear, smell, taste, and feel?			
Do you use action words to describe what happens?			
Do you use descriptive similes and metaphors?			
Do you describe events in the order they happen?			
Have you corrected mistakes in spelling, grammar, and punctuation?			

Directions > Use the notes in your chart and writing plan to revise your draft.

Name _____ Date _____

Writing Report Card

 **Directions** ► Read your revised draft again or ask someone else to read it. Have the person who reads your paper complete the following Report Card. Revise your paper until you have no less than a Very Good Score for each item.

Title of paper: _____

Purpose of paper: ___ **This paper is a descriptive story. It describes** ___

___ **something a friend or relative and I did together.** ___

Person who scores the paper: _____

Score	Writing Goals
	Does this story tell about something that happened to the writer and a friend or relative?
	Are the events that happen in the story in order?
	Does the writer describe what he or she sees, hears, tastes, smells, and feels?
	Does the writer use interesting action words?
	Does the story include descriptive similes and metaphors?
	Are the story's grammar, spelling, and punctuation correct?

☺ Excellent Score   ☆ Very Good Score   + Good Score

✔ Acceptable Score   − Needs Improvement

A Model Paper

A How-to Paper

Build a Newton's Cradle

Sir Isaac Newton was an English mathematician and scientist who lived in the 1600s and 1700s. He published his three laws of motion, which describe how forces affect the motion of an object, in 1687. You can demonstrate one of Newton's laws of motion with an apparatus called a Newton's cradle. The cradle will show that things at rest tend to stay at rest until acted on by an outside force. A Newton's cradle also demonstrates what scientists call the "Principle of Conservation of Energy." That means that energy is never created or destroyed. Energy can change from one form to another, but the total amount of energy stays the same.

It is easier to understand these scientific principles if you use your own Newton's cradle. You need only a few materials to build one. They are:

- 1 ruler marked in inches
- 1 pencil or dowel rod
- scissors
- 5 paper clips
- 5 8-in. pieces of fishing line
- 5 wooden beads

Once you have your materials, you are ready to begin building. Here's how.

First, use your ruler to make five marks on the pencil or dowel rod. The marks should be exactly one inch apart. Be sure the third mark is in the center of the pencil or dowel rod.

Second, use the scissors to score, or cut, a ring around each mark on the pencil or dowel rod. The ring should go all the way around the pencil or rod. Handle the scissors carefully so that you don't cut your skin.

Next, tie a paper clip to one end of each piece of fishing line. Place each paper clip in exactly the same place on each line.

Then, thread one piece of fishing line through the hole in each bead. Each bead will rest on a paper clip.

Now, tie each piece of fishing line around the scored rings on the pencil or dowel rod. The beads must line up exactly and hang evenly.

Use one hand to hold the pencil or rod horizontally. Pull the first bead on one end back. Then release it gently. Observe what happens. The bead you release exerts a force on the other beads.

Now consider the Principle of Conservation of Energy to examine what happens to the beads on your Newton's cradle. Before you released the bead, the bead had one kind of energy called potential energy. When you let the bead fall, the potential energy changed into another kind of energy called kinetic energy. Kinetic energy is the energy of motion.

Wait. There are still more changes in energy. When the first bead hit the second bead, what did you hear? You heard a click. A click is sound energy. Now think about what happens when two things rub together. For example, if you rub your hands together, can you feel your hands getting warmer? The kinetic energy in your hands changes to heat energy. The same thing happens with the beads on your Newton's cradle. As the first bead hits the second bead, energy moves through the beads to the bead at the other end. The bead lifts, swings back, and hits the line of beads. Each time a bead hits another bead, kinetic energy changes to sound and heat energy. Eventually, the kinetic energy changes completely to sound and heat, and the beads stop moving. But don't expect this to happen quickly. The changes of energy are small, so it takes some time for the beads to stop moving.

Now you know how to build a Newton's cradle. You also know how to use the cradle to demonstrate some interesting scientific principles. Try making other Newton's cradles. Use different sizes of dowel rods and string. Change the number of beads, or use metal beads. You might even want to demonstrate your super science skills for the class.

Respond to the Model Paper

Directions ⟩ Write your answers to the following questions or directions.

1. What materials do you need to make a Newton's cradle?

   _____

   _____

2. Why is it important that the beads line up exactly and evenly?

   _____

   _____

3. Why do you need a cord or string?

   _____

   _____

4. In the last paragraph, the writer suggests that you build different kinds of Newton's cradles. Write a paragraph to describe the materials you would use if you could build any kind of Newton's cradle you wanted. Draw a picture to go with your paragraph.

   _____

   _____

   _____

   _____

   _____

   _____

   _____

   _____

Analyze the Model Paper

 **Directions** ⟩ Read "Build a Newton's Cradle" again. As you read, think about why the writer wrote this paper. What did the writer do to help explain how to build a cradle? Write your answers to the following questions or directions.

1. Name at least two things that make this paper a good example of a how-to paper.

   _____

   _____

2. Read the first paragraph again. Why do you think the writer included this paragraph in a how-to paper?

   _____

   _____

3. Why does the writer list the materials you need to make a cradle before telling you how to do it?

   _____

   _____

4. Why does the writer use words like *first, next,* and *then?*

   _____

   _____

5. Read the next-to-the-last paragraph on page 45 again. Draw pictures to go with the words the writer uses to explain the Principle of Conservation of Energy.

Writing Assignment

 **Directions** Think about something you want to tell others how to do. Use this writing plan to help you write.

Writing Plan

> **What will you tell others how to do?**

> **List the materials someone will need.**

> **Write the steps someone should follow in order. Number the steps.**

> **Write some sequence words that help the reader know what to do.**

First Draft

Tips for Writing a How-to Paper:
- Choose one thing to teach someone.
- Focus on a plan.
  1. Think of all the materials someone will need.
  2. Think of all the steps someone will follow.
- Use sequence words in your directions.

First Draft

Directions Use your writing plan as a guide as you write your first draft of a *How-to Paper.*

_____

_____

_____

_____

_____

_____

_____

_____

_____

_____

_____

_____

_____

(Continue on your own paper.)

Name _____ Date _____

Revise the Draft

Directions Use the chart below to help you revise your draft. Check *Yes* or *No* to answer each question in the chart. If you answer *No*, make notes to remind yourself how you can revise, or change, your writing to improve it.

Question	Yes ✔	No ✔	If the answer is no, what will you do to improve your writing?
Does your paper teach someone how to do something?			
Do you use the first paragraph to introduce the project or task?			
Do you include all of the materials someone needs?			
Do you explain all of the steps someone must follow?			
Are the steps in order?			
Do you explain each step clearly so that it is easy to follow?			
Do you use sequence words to help guide your reader?			
Have you corrected mistakes in spelling, grammar, and punctuation?			

Directions Use the notes in your chart and writing plan to revise your draft.

Writing Report Card

 **Directions** ▸ Read your revised draft again or ask someone else to read it. Have the person who reads your paper complete the following Report Card. Revise your paper until you have no less than a Very Good Score for each item.

Title of paper: _____

Purpose of paper: _____**This paper explains how to do something.**_____

Person who scores the paper: _____

Score	Writing Goals
	Does the writer introduce the topic in the first paragraph?
	Does the paper teach someone how to do something?
	Does the paper include the materials someone needs?
	Does the paper explain each step someone will follow?
	Are the steps in order?
	Is each step written clearly to make it easy to follow?
	Are there sequence words to help the reader understand?
	Are the paper's grammar, spelling, and punctuation correct?

☺ Excellent Score   ☆ Very Good Score   + Good Score

✔ Acceptable Score   − Needs Improvement

Name _____   Date _____

A Model Paper

A Compare and Contrast Paper

In-line Skates and Ice Skates

Two fast-moving sports popular with people of all ages are two kinds of skating. They are in-line skating and ice-skating. Whether skaters are on the sidewalk or on the ice, most of them can enjoy hours of fun. That is, of course, if they have the right equipment.

Skaters in both sports use equipment that is alike and different. Both kinds of skates are made for speed. Today's skates let a skater skate well all the time. Skaters can also use their skates in more than one sport. However, certain kinds of skates are made for different uses. They work best when a skater uses the right skate for the right sport. That means, for example, that a hockey player uses skates made for hockey. She can also use them to figure skate. However, in that case, she will probably skate better if she uses skates made for figure skating.

All in-line skates are made for land. So, they all have the same basic features. An in-line skate has a boot that is usually made from plastic. The boot is firm. It holds the skater's ankles comfortably. The boot's lining comes out so it can be washed. On the outside of the boot, there are laces, buckles, or both to fasten the boot.

Ice skates also have a boot, but this boot is made only for ice. The boot is usually made from leather. It provides support for the ankles. It is also designed to be comfortable and warm. The boot's lining is made from a material that helps air move. However, the longer the skater wears the boot, the more likely the skater's feet will perspire. Over time, this can cause a boot to deteriorate, or break down. That makes it important to wipe out the boot after each use.

Both kinds of skates have one or more objects that help the skater move. In-line skates use wheels, usually four. There are three things about the wheels that require the skater's attention. They are size, hardness, and bearings. To check the size of the wheel, the skater measures the wheel's diameter in millimeters (mm). The size of the wheel is important, because the larger it is, the faster it rolls. Most ordinary in-line skates range from 72 mm to 76 mm. The size is marked on the side of the wheel.

The second important feature of the wheel is its hardness. Wheels are made from a kind of plastic. The hardness of the plastic varies and is measured in durometers. A zero durometer represents the softest plastic. One hundred durometers represent the hardest plastic. The harder the plastic, the faster the skater can go.

The last important feature of a wheel is its bearings. Ball bearings are inside the hubs of the wheels. These ball bearings let the wheels roll. So, the better the ball bearings, the faster the wheels roll.

Instead of wheels, ice skates use blades. The blades are attached to the soles of the boot with a screw mount. This mount holds the blade tightly in place.

Blades are made of metal, usually stainless steel. Then they are coated with another metal, such as chrome, nickel, or aluminum. The blade is solid and has a toe pick at the front end. The toe pick lets the skater grip the ice. It also helps the skater take off. There is a ridge that runs along the bottom of the blade. This ridge is called the "hollow." The hollow cuts the ice as the skater glides over it.

Being able to stop is important to every skater. Only in-line skates have brakes. Brake pads are attached to the back of each boot. The skater stops by lifting his or her toes and pressing the brake pad to the ground.

For ice skaters, stopping is another matter. There are no brakes on ice skates. Instead, the skater uses his or her legs and feet to stop. The skater presses on the sides of his or her skates to stop.

In-line skating and ice-skating are alike in some ways and different in others. Their differences make both sports interesting to many skaters. The ways they are alike let skaters skate in both sports. For skaters with the right skates, skating is several sports in one.

Respond to the Model Paper

Directions ▷ Summarize the story by making a chart. Use the chart below to list ways in-line skates and ice skates are alike and different.

**A Compare and Contrast Chart
for
In-line Skates and Ice Skates**

How In-line Skates and Ice Skates Are Alike	How In-line Skates and Ice Skates Are Different

Analyze the Model Paper

 **Directions** ▷ Read "In-line Skates and Ice Skates" again. As you read, think about how the writer achieved his or her purpose for writing. Write your answers to the following questions or directions.

1. When does the writer tell you what this paper is going to be about?

    _____

    _____

    _____

2. Why do you think the writer talks about how in-line skates and ice skates are alike before explaining how they are different?

    _____

    _____

    _____

3. List three differences between in-line skates and ice skates. List them in the order the writer describes them. Explain why you think the writer used this order.

    _____

    _____

    _____

    _____

4. How are the first and last paragraphs related?

    _____

    _____

    _____

    _____

Name _____   Date _____

Writing Assignment

 **Directions** → Think about two sports you would like to write about. Write about how they are alike and how they are different. Use this writing plan to help you write.

Writing Plan

Choose two sports you want to write about. Call them A and B.

A = _____   B = _____

Use what you know, books, or the Internet to learn more about A and B. Learn about three main ideas: where the sports are played, what equipment players need, and the rules. Under each main idea, list what is true only about A in the A circle. List what is true only about B in the B circle. List what is true about both A and B where the two circles overlap.

Main Idea:
Where Are the
Sports Played?

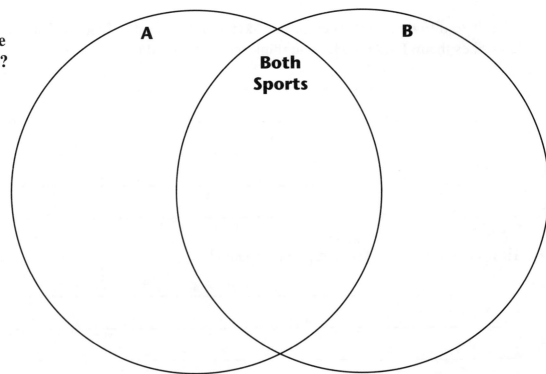

Writing Assignment, page 2

Main Idea: What Equipment
Do Players Need?

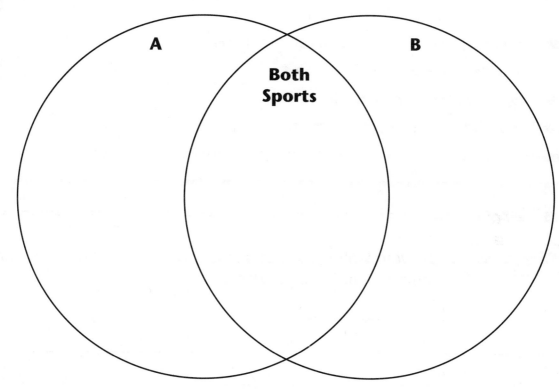

Main Idea:

What Are
the Rules?

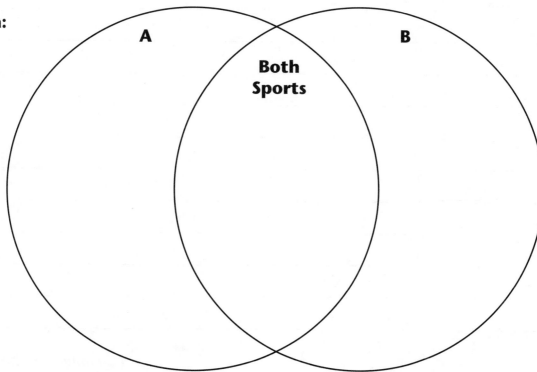

First Draft

Tips for Writing a Compare and Contrast Paper:

- Find information about your sports.
- Organize the information you find into main ideas.
- Use details to explain each main idea.
- Explain how the sports are alike.
- Explain how the sports are different.
- Use your last paragraph to summarize your main ideas in a new way.

First Draft

Directions Use your writing plan as a guide as you write your first draft of a *Compare and Contrast Paper*.

_____

_____

_____

_____

_____

_____

_____

_____

_____

_____

_____

_____

(Continue on your own paper.)

Name _____ Date _____

Revise the Draft

Directions ▷ Use the chart below to help you revise your draft. Check *Yes* or *No* to answer each question in the chart. If you answer *No*, make notes to remind yourself how you can revise, or change, your writing to improve it.

Question	Yes ✔	No ✔	If the answer is no, what will you do to improve your writing?
Do you introduce the sports you will write about in the first paragraph?			
Does your paper explain how two sports are alike?			
Does your paper explain how two sports are different?			
Do you have more than one main idea about each sport?			
Did you organize the main ideas into paragraphs?			
Do you use details to support each main idea?			
Do you summarize the main ideas of your paper in your conclusion?			
Have you corrected mistakes in spelling, grammar, and punctuation?			

Directions ▷ Use the notes in your chart and writing plan to revise your draft.

Writing Report Card

Directions ➤ Read your revised draft again or ask someone else to read it. Have the person who reads your paper complete the following Report Card. Revise your paper until you have no less than a Very Good Score for each item.

Title of paper: _____

Purpose of paper: _____ <u>This paper compares and contrasts two sports.</u> _____

Person who scores the paper:_____

Score	Writing Goals
	Does the writer tell what the paper will be about in the first paragraph?
	Does the paper explain how two sports are alike?
	Does the paper explain how two sports are different?
	Does the writer use more than one main idea to show the important ways the sports are alike and different?
	Does the writer organize the paragraphs in a way that makes sense?
	Does the writer use important details to support each main idea?
	Does the last paragraph summarize what the paper is about?
	Are the paper's grammar, spelling, and punctuation correct?

☺ Excellent Score   ☆ Very Good Score   + Good Score

✔ Acceptable Score   − Needs Improvement

A Model Paper

A Short Report

Why Do Bats Sing?

One day in December 1994, Barbara French began her daily routine. You might be surprised to learn what kind of routine she keeps. She takes care of bats. Barbara's bats are Mexican free-tailed bats (*Tadarida brasiliensis*). The bats she cares for have been hurt and cannot return to the wild. Barbara thought this December day would be like any other, but it wasn't. She got a real surprise. The surprise was the beginning of a scientific discovery.

As Barbara fed the bats, she heard an unfamiliar, bird-like song. She stopped to listen. She heard all of the normal sounds. She recognized Hannah's buzz. Hannah buzzes when she defends her favorite roosting spot. Then Barbara heard Wheatley's squeal. She could tell that another bat had chased him away from the mealworm tray. Barbara also heard the chirp Amy makes when she wants to be fed by hand. But she had never heard this new song before.

Barbara decided to solve the mystery. Whenever she heard the song, Barbara popped her head into the bat cage. As soon as her head was inside the cage, the singing stopped. It took Barbara two weeks to find the singing bat. The singer was Hank, an adult male. He seemed to be singing to a small group of females in his roosting pocket. A roosting pocket is a handmade fabric pouch, or bag, in the bats' cage.

In the following weeks, the male bats became unusually bold and ready to fight. They chased each other all the time. Free-tailed bats usually like the company of other bats, so Barbara thought this behavior was odd. Ordinarily, the bats like to roost together.

Barbara was worried by this change in the bats' behavior. Her familiar little bat colony was suddenly very different. The bats had been happy with each other for the past year. Of course, they sometimes squabbled, pushed, shoved, and swatted at each other. However, these were normal bat behaviors. Plus, the bats always settled their differences quickly. They didn't hurt each other. The bat that started a fight usually tried to end the fight. He or she would snuggle up with the other bats. It was as if the bat wanted to say it was sorry. The entire colony seemed to work together to keep the peace. However, Hank was different.

One day Barbara watched Hank attack Joshua, another bat. Hank darted from his pocket. He buzzed loudly and chased Joshua around the cage. Barbara decided Joshua had probably moved too near Hank's territory. Before Barbara could stop him, Hank caught Joshua and snagged his ear. Hank's anger bothered Barbara, but what followed really upset her. Moments after she had rescued Joshua, he squeezed out of her hand. Joshua zoomed back into Hank's territory. Joshua seemed ready to fight back.

Because she didn't understand the bats' new behaviors, Barbara decided to ask for help. She called Amanda Lollar. Amanda is a licensed expert in the care of captive Mexican free-tailed bats. Amanda told Barbara that Hank was probably "singing to his women." Amanda also told Barbara to watch for pups that would probably be born during the summer. Barbara was surprised that the explanation was so simple. The bats that Barbara cared for would never be wild again. Their problems made it impossible for them to care for themselves. Barbara didn't think that the bats were strong enough to have healthy pups.

The problems were not over. Barbara and the other bats found Hank's behavior too hard to manage. Hank fought with other males all the time. He bit Joshua's ear again. He even tried to attack Barbara as she fed a female.

Barbara noticed something new. Three females that had been roosting with Hank suddenly began eating more. They ate everything Barbara fed them and wanted more.

Finally, Hank's singing stopped. The females left Hank and moved into Wheatley's roosting area. Eventually, Hank became himself again. The Hank problem was solved, but a Wheatley problem began. Wheatley began to guard the females that were expecting babies. Wheatley became as fierce as Hank had been.

In June, as Barbara was feeding the bats, she saw a little, pink pup about the size of a walnut. Although the baby was very young, he was able to follow his mother around inside the roosting pocket. Twelve days later, Barbara saw the birth of a second pup. This baby was born with his eyes open. He was able to lick his tiny wings clean within minutes after birth.

Barbara learned a lot from her experience with her bats. So did scientists who study bats. Barbara was able to give scientists information they had never had before. Hank's music wasn't a mystery anymore. Neither was Wheatley's protective behavior. Thanks to Barbara and her bats, scientists now know much more about the mating behaviors of Mexican free-tailed bats.

Respond to the Model Paper

Directions Write your answers to the following questions or directions.

1. Why was Barbara surprised the first time she heard a bat sing?

   _____

   _____

2. Why was Barbara surprised when the male bats became more willing to fight?

   _____

   _____

3. Why did Barbara contact Amanda Lollar?

   _____

   _____

4. Write a paragraph to summarize the report. Use these questions to help you
   write your summary:

   • What are the main ideas in this report?
   • How did Amanda explain Hank's behavior?
   • What did scientists learn from Barbara's experience?

   _____

   _____

   _____

   _____

   _____

   _____

   _____

   _____

Analyze the Model Paper

Directions > Read "Why Do Bats Sing?" again. As you read, think about the main ideas the writer tells about. Write your answers to the following questions.

1. Which paragraph did the writer use to tell you what this report was going to be about?

   _____

   _____

2. Read the second paragraph again. What details did the writer use to explain why the singing was unusual?

   _____

   _____

3. Read the fifth and sixth paragraphs again. How does the sixth paragraph support the fifth paragraph?

   _____

   _____

   _____

   _____

4. How is the first paragraph related to the last paragraph?

   _____

   _____

   _____

   _____

   _____

Writing Assignment

Directions In a short report, writers write about one topic. They find information about the topic. Then they use the information to choose the main ideas for their report. They also choose details to help explain each main idea. Write a short report about a science topic that interests you. Your idea might even come from the report "Why Do Bats Sing?" Use this writing plan to help you write.

Writing Plan

The topic of this paper is:

_____

Main Idea of Paragraph 1: _____

Detail: _____

Detail: _____

Detail: _____

Main Idea of Paragraph 2: _____

Detail: _____

Detail: _____

Detail: _____

Main Idea of Paragraph 3: _____

Detail: _____

Detail: _____

Detail: _____

First Draft

Tips for Writing a Short Report:

- Find information about your topic.
- Take notes about main ideas important to your topic.
- Take notes about important details for each main idea.
- Organize the main ideas and details into paragraphs.
- Put paragraphs in a logical order.
- Use the last paragraph to summarize your report.

First Draft

Directions > Use your writing plan as a guide as you write your first draft of a *Short Report.*

_____

_____

_____

_____

_____

_____

_____

_____

_____

_____

_____

(Continue on your own paper.)

Revise the Draft

Directions ▷ Use the chart below to help you revise your draft. Check *Yes* or *No* to answer each question in the chart. If you answer *No*, make notes to remind yourself how you can revise, or change, your writing to improve it.

Question	Yes ✔	No ✔	If the answer is no, what will you do to improve your writing?
Does your report focus on one topic?			
Do you introduce your topic in the first paragraph?			
Do you have more than one main idea to explain your topic?			
Do you organize your main ideas into paragraphs?			
Do you include details to explain each main idea?			
Do you use your last paragraph to summarize your report?			
Have you corrected mistakes in spelling, grammar, and punctuation?			

Directions ▷ Use the notes in your chart and writing plan to revise your draft.

Name _____ Date _____

Writing Report Card

Directions ⟩ Read your revised draft again or ask someone else to read it. Have the person who reads your paper complete the following Report Card. Revise your paper until you have no less than a Very Good Score for each item.

Title of paper: _____

Purpose of paper: _____ **This paper is a short report.** _____

Person who scores the paper: _____

Score	Writing Goals
	Does this short report focus on one topic?
	Does the writer introduce the topic of this paper in the first paragraph?
	Does the writer use more than one main idea to explain the topic?
	Are main ideas organized into paragraphs?
	Are there details to explain each main idea?
	Does the report "stick" to the topic?
	Does the last paragraph summarize the report?
	Are the report's grammar, spelling, and punctuation correct?

☺ Excellent Score   ☆ Very Good Score   + Good Score

✔ Acceptable Score   — Needs Improvement

A Model Paper

A Persuasive Letter

121 Sparrow Lane
Mason City, Iowa

November 12, 2002

Carlos Gonzales
P.O. Box 122
Des Moines, Iowa

Dear Carlos,

Everyone here is fine and looking forward to the Thanksgiving holiday. School is really hard. All of us at school are going nuts. Even Mom and Dad are ready for a break. We can't wait for the holiday. I just wish you were going to be here to share it with us.

Mom said that you called Thursday night while I was at play practice. Did I tell you that I got the lead in the school play? It's pretty good, I guess. Anyway, I'm sorry that I didn't get to talk to you. Maybe I could have convinced you to come home for Thanksgiving. Mom said that you're going home with your roommate. Where is Aspen, Colorado, anyway?

Everyone will be here—Abuelita, Abuelito, Uncle Eduardo, Aunt Anna, Michael, Mom, Dad, and of course, me. Everybody will be here but you. I don't know if you've thought much about Abuelito lately. He's getting old, you know. Nanny told Mom that the last time Aunt Anna visited, Abuelito couldn't remember her name. I bet he'd remember you, though. Abuelito always really loved you. Thanksgiving would be a perfect time to see him, don't you agree?

It's been a while since we've talked. Since you went away to school, I haven't had anyone to talk to about those really personal things. You know what I mean. I don't want you to worry or anything. I don't have a big, horrible problem right now. But you never know when one's going to come up, and then what will I do? We've never talked about how to handle personal emergencies while you're away. It sure seems like Thanksgiving would be a perfect time to talk about that.

Oh, I just thought of another reason you should come home for Thanksgiving. I have two words for you—football game. How can we have our traditional family game if you aren't here? We don't have enough players without you. Do you remember last year when I made that extra point just seconds before we were called into dinner? I think that was the best Thanksgiving game we've ever had, don't you? I wonder. Does your roommate's family play football on Thanksgiving? Does he know that you led your high school team to the district playoffs last year?

I think I've almost run out of things to say. Wait, I remember one other thing. Mrs. Sanchez visited the other day. I heard her tell Mom that Marcie was coming home for Thanksgiving. Wow. I haven't seen Marcie since you and she took me camping right before school started. That was a great time. Just thinking about it makes me want to go camping again. I wonder if Marcie would like to put up a tent in the backyard. We could have Thanksgiving dinner out there. Of course, camping might not be as much fun if it's just the two of us. It wouldn't feel right without you.

Well, Carlos, I think I'm at the end of this letter. I don't know what else to write. I sure would like to see you at Thanksgiving. It won't be the same if you're not here. Of course, I'm not trying to pressure you. It's your decision. I know you'll do the right thing. Besides, you're probably not as crazy about Abuelita's famous homemade cranberry sauce as I am. And I can't remember if icebox lemon pie is still your favorite dessert. I'm making one, you know. Oh, well. I bet the food in Aspen is pretty good, too.

I really am going to say goodbye now. I sure miss you. I hope you have a great Thanksgiving. I'll do the best I can without you.

> Your best and only sister,
> Daniella

P.S. Does your roommate like icebox lemon pie? I can make a pumpkin pie if he likes that better.

Respond to the Model Paper

Directions ➤ Write your answers to the following questions or directions.

1. Why is Daniella writing to her brother?

   _____

   _____

2. List the reasons Daniella gives to explain why her brother should come home.

   _____

   _____

   _____

   _____

3. Why do you think Daniella mentions Marcie in her letter?

   _____

   _____

4. Write a paragraph to summarize the main points Daniella makes in her letter. Use these questions to help you write your summary:

   • Why is Daniella writing?
   • What reasons does Daniella give her brother to come home for Thanksgiving?

   _____

   _____

   _____

   _____

   _____

   _____

Analyze the Model Paper

 **Directions** Read the persuasive letter from Daniella again. As you read, think about why she wrote this letter. Write your answers to the following questions or directions.

1. Read the first paragraph again. Write the sentence that tells you what this letter is about.

   _____

   _____

2. Read the third paragraph again. Why do you think Daniella wrote this paragraph?

   _____

   _____

   _____

3. How do you think Daniella's brother will feel after reading this letter? Why?

   _____

   _____

   _____

   _____

4. Read the postscript (P.S.) again. Why do you think Daniella added this message?

   _____

   _____

   _____

   _____

   _____

Writing Assignment

Directions > In a persuasive letter, a writer tries to convince someone or a group of people to do something. The writer tries to make the reader feel a certain emotion about the topic he or she writes about. Write a persuasive letter to a friend to convince him or her to spend a weekend with you. Use this writing plan to help you write.

Writing Plan

1. Write your address.

2. Write the date.

3. Write your friend's name and address.

4. Write a polite greeting, or salutation.

5. What will you say in the first paragraph to let your friend know why you are writing?

6. Complete the chart.

Main Points You Will Present	Supporting Details You Will Use

7. Use your last paragraph to write a conclusion. Summarize the important points you made.

8. Choose a friendly closing.

9. Sign your name.

First Draft

Tips for Writing a Persuasive Letter:

- Use a strong beginning to grab your reader's attention.
- Make your purpose for writing clear to the reader.
- Use examples that will appeal to your reader's emotions.
- Organize your examples from least important to most important.
- Use a strong ending that leaves your reader convinced you are right.

First Draft

Directions ▷ Use your writing plan as a guide for writing your first draft of a *Persuasive Letter.*

_____

_____

_____

_____

_____

_____

_____

_____

_____

_____

_____

_____

(Continue on your own paper.)

Revise the Draft

Directions ⟩ Use the chart below to help you revise your draft. Check *Yes* or *No* to answer each question in the chart. If you answer *No*, make notes to remind yourself how you can revise, or change, your writing to improve it.

Question	Yes ✔	No ✔	If the answer is no, what will you do to improve your writing?
Is the purpose of this letter clear?			
Does the first paragraph grab your reader's attention?			
Do you use specific examples to convince your reader?			
Are the examples you use in order from the least to the most important?			
Do you appeal to your reader's emotions?			
Do you use the last paragraph to restate your opinion in a convincing way?			
Have you corrected mistakes in spelling, grammar, and punctuation?			

Directions ⟩ Use the notes in your chart and writing plan to revise your draft.

Name _____   Date _____

Writing Report Card

 **Directions** Read your revised draft again or ask someone else to read it. Have the person who reads your paper complete the following Report Card. Revise your paper until you have no less than a Very Good Score for each item.

Title of paper: _____

Purpose of paper: _____ **This is a persuasive letter.** _____

Person who scores the paper:_____

Score	Writing Goals
	Is the writer's purpose for writing clear?
	Does the writer grab the reader's attention in the first paragraph?
	Does the writer use specific examples to convince the reader?
	Are examples presented in order from the least to the most important?
	Does the writer appeal to the reader's emotions?
	Does the last paragraph leave the reader convinced the writer is right?
	Are the letter's grammar, spelling, and punctuation correct?

☺ Excellent Score   ☆ Very Good Score   + Good Score

✔ Acceptable Score   — Needs Improvement

A Model Paper

A Persuasive Movie Review

Bernie, the Laughing Ogre

If a story needs one hero, one princess in distress, and one villain, or evil force, to be a fairy tale, then *Bernie, the Laughing Ogre* may be one of the funniest fairy tales you've ever seen. That's right, the word is seen, not heard. Because *Bernie, the Laughing Ogre* is a movie, and its characters are unlike any fairy tale characters you've ever met before.

Let's start with the hero, Bernie. Bernie is tall, but definitely not handsome. In fact, he's a chubby, purple giant with too much hair. Most of the time, too much hair on a giant isn't a problem. But Bernie's hair grows in all the wrong places. There's hair between his toes and fingers. There's even hair growing from his nose and ears, but there's no hair on his head or body. Bernie is bald.

There's something else that makes Bernie an uncommon hero. He's ticklish. A single scratch on his bald, purple skin makes Bernie lose control. He falls to the ground, laughing and gasping for air. Bernie knows this is unacceptable behavior for a giant. In fact, his giant friends have threatened to kick Bernie out of their drama club if he can't be more serious. Bernie wants to act like other giants, but he can't help himself.

To be safe, Bernie never goes into the nearby village where he might rub up against the moles. That may not seem so funny, but you need to remember that moles are hairy and blind. They use their whiskers to see. Their short, stubby whiskers are always moving about. If you're a bald, ticklish giant like Bernie, you can see why moles might be a problem. In fact, Bernie avoids moles altogether. That includes princess moles.

The princess in this story is no ordinary fairy-tale princess. For one thing, she's a mole. For the second thing, she's not really in distress. She's used to the dull, dark castle where she lives. She's also used to the boring dragon that holds her captive. Princess Stella has learned to make herself laugh, but only when the dragon isn't around. Nothing makes the dragon angrier than laughter. The first time the princess laughed, the dragon shook and shivered. Steam came from his ears. His skin turned from blue to red. This made the princess laugh, too. That made the dragon even more furious. The princess soon realized that of all the dragons in the world, she got the one without a sense of humor. That's when she decided to find a way out of the castle. Plus, she worried about the moles in her village. What was the villain Manco doing to them?

Manco is like most of the villains you read about in fairy tales. He never smiles unless he's being wicked. Nothing makes him happier than making someone else unhappy. That's why he let the dragon into the village to kidnap the princess. He knew that once the princess was gone, everyone in the village would be sad. That's where Bernie's problem begins.

Most of the time, no one comes near the dark, unfriendly forest where Bernie lives. Until the moles come, that is. You see, some of the moles decide they need a giant to help them rescue their princess and bring laughter back to the village. Their first stop is Bernie's forest.

Unless Bernie agrees to help, the moles tell him more moles will come. Bernie has no choice. He must say yes or risk becoming the laughingstock of giants everywhere. So, Bernie agrees to rescue the princess if the moles promise to return home. The moles promise, but that's not exactly what happens.

I could tell you more, but I don't want to spoil the surprises that fill this movie. Don't think about how Bernie helps all of those hairy, whiskered moles rescue the princess. Don't imagine what the dragon does the first time he hears Bernie laugh. You'll see how Bernie handles these problems when you see the movie. Right now, I'd like to talk about something else that's going to make you love this fairy tale.

Bernie, the Laughing Ogre, the movie, is an example of the best of computer technology. The people who brought these characters to life have done something extraordinary. Each character walks, talks, and looks like a real living thing. When Bernie smiles, you see wrinkles in his bald skin. When the wind blows, you see each mole whisker twitch. When the dragon breathes fire, you almost feel the flames. Characters look so real, you're sure they are.

There are hundreds of reasons why you should see *Bernie, the Laughing Ogre*. There's not a single reason not to see it. This story isn't like the fairy tales you read when you were a child. It will make you laugh. You'll also be amazed by the computer magic that made this movie. See the movie now. Then you can make plans to see it a second time because I'm sure you will.

Respond to the Model Paper

Directions ➤ Write your answers to the following questions or directions.

1. Why is the hero uncommon?

   _____

   _____

2. Besides the hero, who are the other important characters in this movie?

   _____

   _____

3. Describe the plot of the movie in one or two sentences.

   _____

   _____

   _____

4. Write a paragraph to summarize *Bernie, the Laughing Ogre*. Use these questions to help you write your summary:

   • What is the purpose of this paper?
   • What reasons does the writer give for seeing this movie?

   _____

   _____

   _____

   _____

   _____

   _____

   _____

   _____

Analyze the Model Paper

 **Directions** Read *Bernie, the Laughing Ogre* again. As you read, think about the reasons the writer gives to convince readers to see this movie. Write your answers to the following questions.

1. How does the writer use the first paragraph to grab a reader's attention?

    _____

    _____

    _____

    _____

2. Read paragraph nine again. Why do you think the writer included this paragraph?

    _____

    _____

    _____

    _____

3. The writer uses most of the review to talk about the characters and plot. Why do you think the writer includes paragraph ten?

    _____

    _____

    _____

    _____

4. What do the first and last paragraphs have in common?

    _____

    _____

    _____

    _____

Name _____ Date _____

Writing Assignment

 **Directions** ⟩ In a persuasive movie review, writers try to convince readers to watch a movie. What's your favorite movie? Write a persuasive movie review to convince your friends to see this movie. Use this writing plan to help you write.

Writing Plan

What is the name of the movie you will review?

_____

Write reasons your friends should see this movie. Write details to support each reason.

Reason #1

_____

_____

Details to support Reason #1

_____

_____

_____

_____

Reason #2

_____

_____

Details to support Reason #2

_____

_____

_____

_____

Reason #3

_____

_____

Details to support Reason #3

_____

_____

_____

_____

Reason #4

_____

_____

Details to support Reason #4

_____

_____

_____

_____

First Draft

Tips for Writing a Persuasive Movie Review:

- Make sure you have a strong opinion.
- Give good reasons to support your opinion.
- Give important details that support each reason.
- Grab your reader's attention in the first paragraph.
- Restate your opinion in the last paragraph.

First Draft

Directions ⟩ Use your writing plan as a guide for writing your first draft of a *Persuasive Movie Review.*

_____

_____

_____

_____

_____

_____

_____

_____

_____

_____

_____

_____

_____

(Continue on your own paper.)

Revise the Draft

Directions > Use the chart below to help you revise your draft. Check *Yes* or *No* to answer each question in the chart. If you answer *No*, make notes to remind yourself how you can revise, or change, your writing to improve it.

Question	Yes ✔	No ✔	If the answer is no, what will you do to improve your writing?
Do you use your first paragraph to grab the reader's attention?			
Do you make it clear that you have a strong opinion?			
Do you give good reasons to support your opinion?			
Do you include details that help support each reason?			
Do you restate your opinion in the last paragraph?			
Does this review make your reader want to see the movie?			
Have you corrected mistakes in spelling, grammar, and punctuation?			

Directions > Use the notes in your chart and writing plan to revise your draft.

Writing Report Card

Directions Read your revised draft again or ask someone else to read it. Have the person who reads your paper complete the following Report Card. Revise your paper until you have no less than a Very Good Score for each item.

Title of paper: _____

Purpose of paper: _____ This paper is a persuasive movie review. _____

Person who scores the paper:_____

Score	Writing Goals
	Does the first paragraph grab the reader's attention?
	Is the writer's opinion clearly stated?
	Does the writer give good reasons for his or her opinion?
	Are there details to support each reason?
	Does the writer restate his or her opinion in the last paragraph?
	Does this review make you want to see the movie?
	Are the report's grammar, spelling, and punctuation correct?

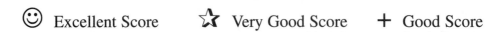

☺ Excellent Score   ☆ Very Good Score   + Good Score

✔ Acceptable Score   − Needs Improvement

A Model Paper

A Persuasive Essay

Why Americans Should Celebrate Cinco de Mayo

In Spanish, the name *Cinco de Mayo* means the 5th of May. It is a Mexican holiday that all Americans should observe. The holiday celebrates an historic victory in the city of Puebla, Mexico, on May 5, 1862. Two groups of soldiers fought each other. A small Mexican army of soldiers and ordinary citizens battled against French forces. The French forces had better equipment and training, but the Mexican forces won the battle.

The Mexican army's victory was small. It did not end French control of Mexico. In fact, the French would conquer and rule Mexico for five more years. But the Battle of Puebla was important. It showed that ordinary Mexican citizens could fight against a powerful foreign force and win.

Why were French forces in Mexico? When the Battle of Puebla happened, Mexico was in trouble. The Mexican-American War had ended in 1848, and Mexico owed other countries a lot of money. The national treasury was almost empty. So in 1861, Mexican President Benito Juárez said that Mexico would not pay what it owed for two years. He promised to pay later, but France, Spain, and England did not want to wait. Each country sent people to collect the money Mexico owed them. In time, the Spanish and English worked out an agreement with President Juárez. They went back, but the French didn't.

Napoleon III of France wanted to take over Mexico and build a French empire. He made Maximilian the new ruler of his empire. He sent French troops to take control.

The French feared no one. They had not lost a single battle in 50 years. The French thought the Mexicans would give up without a fight, but they were wrong.

Texas-born General Ignacio Zaragoza waited for the French forces to come. He was ordered to defend the city of Puebla. The general had 2,000 troops and some loyal Puebla citizens. These poor people brought their farm tools to use as weapons.

The French soldiers charged the city. After only two hours, the battle ended. Many French soldiers had been killed or wounded. Despite the odds against them, the Mexican army defeated the most powerful army in the world. Their victory strengthened the pride of the Mexican people. Their success on May 5, 1862, brought Mexicans together. They were determined to force the French out of their land.

The victory at the Battle of Puebla was also important for Americans. While the French moved toward Mexico City, the capital, President Juárez fled to northern Mexico. There he set up a temporary but powerful government to fight the French. The government's position in northern Mexico prevented the French army from getting supplies to Confederate rebels during the American Civil War. Mexican bravery gave the North another year to strengthen its military. In July 1863, little more than one year after the Battle of Puebla, Northern forces defeated the Confederates at the Battle of Gettysburg.

After the Civil War, President Lincoln told the French to get out of Mexico. He sent General Phil Sheridan and Union soldiers to the border between Texas and Mexico. There Sheridan gave Mexican troops the supplies they needed to control the French. In early 1867, Napoleon took his troops out of Mexico. The brave Mexican people controlled their country again.

Cinco de Mayo is not a celebration of Mexico's independence. It marks a day when Mexicans discovered how strong they are. Cinco de Mayo is a day that shows national pride. Today, many Mexican-Americans have parades and festivals on Cinco de Mayo. They play traditional music and dance. They share traditional food, arts, and crafts.

Some historians think other Americans should celebrate, too. If Mexico hadn't forced the French out of their country, the American Civil War might have ended differently. If the Confederates had won the war, the United States might be two countries instead of one. This is enough reason for Americans to celebrate Cinco de Mayo. There is also another good reason.

By recognizing Cinco de Mayo, Americans could learn more about people who showed great courage. They could appreciate what Americans owe those few, brave Mexican soldiers who fought in 1862.

Name _____ Date _____

Respond to the Model Paper

Directions ▶ Write your answers to the following questions or directions.

1. Why were French forces in Mexico?

_____

_____

2. Why did the French forces expect to win the Battle of Puebla?

_____

_____

3. What made the Mexican army at Puebla unusual?

_____

_____

4. Write a paragraph to summarize the essay. Use these questions to help you write your summary:

   • What are the main points the writer makes in this essay?
   • Why should Mexican-Americans celebrate Cinco de Mayo?
   • Why should all Americans celebrate Cinco de Mayo?

_____

_____

_____

_____

_____

_____

_____

Analyze the Writer's Model

 **Directions** Read "Why Americans Should Celebrate Cinco de Mayo" again. As you read, think about the main ideas the writer discusses. Write your answers to the following questions or directions.

1. Write the sentence in the first paragraph that tells what the writer wants to persuade people to do.

   _____

   _____

2. Read the eighth and ninth paragraphs again. Why do you think the writer discusses the American Civil War in this essay?

   _____

   _____

3. Read the last two paragraphs again. What is the writer trying to do in these paragraphs?

   _____

   _____

4. How are the first and last paragraphs related?

   _____

   _____

   _____

   _____

   _____

   _____

   _____

Writing Assignment

Before a writer begins to write a persuasive essay, he or she forms an opinion. This opinion becomes the writer's purpose for writing. Then the writer gives specific reasons why the reader should have the same opinion.

 **Directions** ⟩ Write a persuasive essay about a topic that is important to you. State your opinion clearly. Also offer important reasons for this opinion. Use this writing plan to help you write.

Writing Plan

What will the topic of your essay be?

_____   ◀·▶   **What is your opinion on this topic?**

_____

Reason 1

_____ _____ _____

◀·▶

Why? Support your reason.

_____ _____ _____

Reason 2

_____ _____ _____

◀·▶

Why? Support your reason.

_____ _____ _____

Reason 3

_____ _____ _____

◀·▶

Why? Support your reason.

_____ _____ _____

First Draft

Tips for Writing a Persuasive Essay:
- Grab your reader's attention in the first paragraph.
- State your opinion clearly.
- Support your opinion with clear examples.
- Present your examples from least important to most important.
- Use the last paragraph to summarize your essay.
- Use your last paragraph to leave the reader convinced you are right.

First Draft

Directions ➤ Use your writing plan as a guide for writing your first draft of a *Persuasive Essay*.

_____

_____

_____

_____

_____

_____

_____

_____

_____

_____

_____

(Continue on your own paper.)

Name _____   Date _____

Revise the Draft

Directions > Use the chart below to help you revise your draft. Check *Yes* or *No* to answer each question in the chart. If you answer *No*, make notes to remind yourself how you can revise, or change, your writing to improve it.

Question	Yes ✔	No ✔	If the answer is no, what will you do to improve your writing?
Do you use your first paragraph to grab the reader's attention?			
Do you have a clear opinion?			
Do you include strong reasons that support your opinion?			
Do you organize your reasons from least to most important?			
Do you restate your opinion in the last paragraph?			
Do you use your last paragraph to leave your reader convinced that you are right?			
Have you corrected mistakes in spelling, grammar, and punctuation?			

Directions > Use the notes in your chart and writing plan to revise your draft.

Name _____ Date _____

Writing Report Card

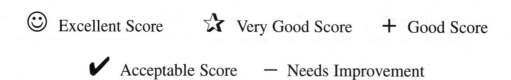**Directions** ➤ Read your revised draft again or ask someone else to read it. Have the person who reads your paper complete the following Report Card. Revise your paper until you have no less than a Very Good Score for each item.

Title of paper: _____

Purpose of paper: ___**This paper is a persuasive essay.**_____

Person who scores the paper:_____

Score	Writing Goals
	Does the writer grab your attention right away?
	Is the writer's opinion absolutely clear?
	Does the writer include examples that support his or her opinion?
	Are the examples organized from least to most important?
	Does the last paragraph restate the writer's opinion in a new way?
	Is the essay convincing?
	Are the essay's grammar, spelling, and punctuation correct?

☺ Excellent Score   ☆ Very Good Score   + Good Score

✔ Acceptable Score   − Needs Improvement

Writing Skills: Grade 6, Answer Key

Answers to some questions may vary, but examples are provided here to give you an idea of how students may respond. Encourage students to share, discuss, and evaluate their answers, particularly their summaries. Also, encourage students to answer all questions in complete sentences.

page 22

1. This story's theme is "friendship" because the story tells how two girls figured out that their friendship was more important than a contest. (Help students support their answers with details from the story.)

2. The writer tells us that Maria was like a sister and gives examples of things that she and Maria did together. The writer also didn't want Maria to withdraw from the yearbook contest. (Look for a clear understanding of the girls' friendship in students' answers. Be sure students include details from the narrative to support their understanding.)

3. Be sure students correctly summarize the significant events of the story, paraphrasing as needed. Summaries should be organized in a thoughtful way, with the main ideas and important details clearly presented. Spelling, punctuation, capitalization, and grammar should be correct.

page 23

1. The writer uses words like *I*, *me*, and *my* to show that she is writing about her personal experiences.

2. The writer introduces the problem in this paragraph. Later we learn that both girls have entered the yearbook contest, and they are afraid that it will hurt their friendship if one of them wins.

3. Both Maria and the writer decide to leave their designs in the contest. They agree that they will remain friends regardless of who wins.

4. The writer tells us that Maria gave her the winning design as a birthday present. This lets us know that Maria won the contest.

page 30

1. The writer learned how to swim.

2. The main setting for this story is the Llano River. The cool river has fast rapids, shallow places, and deep swimming holes that feel good when the hot sun is beating down. (Look for an understanding of setting. Help students use vivid, descriptive words that evoke a clear image of the setting.)

3. In the second paragraph, the writer tells us that J.W. is loud, funny, and a real pain.

4. The writer is surprised when Donnie offers to teach her to swim, so they probably don't do a lot of things together. You can tell he cares about her, though, because he talks to her when she is sitting by herself and he is patient with her as she practices each step. I think the writer trusts Donnie and looks up to him. (Help students form a conclusion and support it with examples.)

5. Check to see that students summarize the significant events of the story. Summaries should be organized in a thoughtful way, with the main ideas and important details clearly presented.

page 31

1. The writer uses dialogue and vivid descriptions to show emotion.

2. Reading exactly what J.W. says instead of a description helps us understand why the writer was so embarrassed.

3. The writer adds funny comments to help readers picture what is going on and to help us understand her personality. Humor keeps the reader interested in the story.

4. For the most part, the writer uses dialogue to help the reader picture J.W. She gives examples of how he teased her and how he complimented her on learning to swim. She also gives examples of how she was feeling because of the teasing, including having to build up her courage to go to the river although J.W. was there, and not wanting to go out in the river where J.W. and her other cousins were playing.

page 38

1. The writer uses interesting words, similes, and metaphors to describe what Cole and his dad saw, heard, felt, and did. (Look for an understanding of the elements of a descriptive narrative.)

2. Cole traced the stitching on his bag. His mom was relieved when Cole's dad telephoned. (Check to see that students address the entire question.)

3. The writer tells us that Cole reassures his dad that he's not upset about the late start to the weekend. Cole tells his dad that he loves the farm and the house. (Encourage students to include specific details from the story, paraphrasing when possible.)

4. Answers will vary. Check drawings.

5. Guide students in summarizing the significant events of the story. Summaries should be organized in a thoughtful way, with the main ideas and important details clearly presented.

page 39

1. "Their red and yellow heads moved up and down like fishing bobs on a lake." "The creek babbled like a child."

2. "The highway was a gray stripe through green countryside."

3. Some interesting verbs included *sliced, bowed, babbled, sparkled, swallowed, groaned, squeezed,* and *ignored.*

4. Drawings should show the interior of a farmhouse, covered with dust and spider webs. Cole should be in the room, with his dad holding his elbow.

5. Answers will vary. Look for descriptive language that expresses the five senses, comparisons, varied sentence length, and personal style, or voice.

page 46

1. You will need the following materials to make a Newton's cradle: a ruler marked in inches, 1 pencil or dowel rod, a pair of scissors, 5 paper clips, 5 8-inch pieces of fishing line, and 5 wooden beads. (Guide students in converting the bulleted list of materials into a sentence.)

2. The beads must line up exactly and evenly in order to hit each other and transfer energy. (Encourage students to draw conclusions based on the information provided in the paper. Sketching the finished Newton's cradle may help students determine the answer.)

3. The string (in this example, fishing line) holds the beads and lets them swing freely. (Guide students in drawing conclusions based on the information provided in the paper. A sketch may help students determine the answer.)

4. If I could, I would build a life-sized Newton's cradle. For the frame, I would use a backyard swing set with all the swings taken off. I would use four old bowling balls as the "beads." They would all need to be the same weight, but they could be different colors. I would ask my dad to help me drill 1-inch holes through the bowling balls with his electric drill. Then, I would find a long rope 1 inch thick. I would use a yardstick to measure the rope into four 5-foot-long pieces. Then, I'd ask my dad to help me cut it. I'd use the pieces of rope to hang the bowling balls on the frame. (Help students make sure they have included all the materials they need. Pictures should match the details provided in the students' paragraphs.)

page 47

1. The writer states the purpose of the paper clearly, lists materials, and gives step-by-step instructions.

2. A Newton's cradle is used to demonstrate scientific principles. If the writer had not included the first paragraph, we might know how to make a Newton's cradle, but we wouldn't know what to do with it or why it is interesting.

3. Listing the materials before giving the directions helps readers make sure they have everything they need before they start building the cradle.

4. The writer uses sequence words such as *first, next,* and *then* to help you understand the order of the steps. These words also help you find your place in the process quickly.

5. Answers may vary. Pictures should illustrate moving beads. Pictures or labels should explain the change from kinetic energy to sound and heat energy.

page 54

Guide students in organizing the information in a clear manner.

How In-line Skates and Ice Skates Are Alike: Both in-line skates and ice skates are built for speed.; The way skates are made today lets skaters skate well all the time.; Skates can be used in more than one sport.; The boots of both in-line and ice skates support the ankles firmly and comfortably.; Both types of skates have devices that help them move.

How In-line Skates and Ice Skates Are Different: In-line skates are used on land while ice skates are made for ice.; The boots of in-line skates are made of plastic, with a liner that can be removed and washed. Ice skates, however, have boots made of leather. The lining lets air move, but it must be wiped clean each time you use the skates because it cannot be taken out.; In-line skates have wheels, usually four, which make them move. The fastest in-line skates have wheels that are bigger (about 76 mm), harder (up to 100 durometers), and have good ball bearings. Ice skates, on the other hand, use blades to move. Blades are solid metal, usually stainless steel coated with chrome, nickel, or aluminum. Blades have a toe pick to help the skater take off and a ridge called a "hollow" that cuts the ice.; Skaters using in-line skates have brakes at the back of each boot to help them stop, but ice-skaters have to use their legs and feet to press down on the sides of their skates to stop.

page 55

1. The writer introduces the topic of the paper in the first paragraph.

2. The similarities are clear and easy to explain, so the writer describes those first.

3. The first difference is how the boots of in-line skates and ice skates are made. The boots of in-line skates are usually made of firm plastic, while ice skate boots are made of leather. Another difference is that in-line skates use wheels, but ice skates use blades. The third difference is related to stopping. In-line skates have brakes, but ice skates don't. I think the writer presented the differences in this order because he or she could talk about how the boots are made, then describe how they move when you're wearing them. When you're skating, the last thing you do is stop, so it makes sense to discuss that last.

4. The first paragraph introduces the topic of the paper. The last paragraph summarizes the paper's topic.

page 63

1. Barbara was surprised because she had heard the bats make lots of sounds, including buzzes, squeals, and chirps, but she had never heard them sing like a bird before. (Help students include all the pertinent information in their answers.)

2. Usually, the bats liked to roost together. Sometimes they had little fights, but they always got over them quickly and made up with each other. All this made Barbara curious about why the bats were fighting more often. (Check to see if students included all significant details.)

3. Amanda Lollar is a licensed expert in the care of Mexican free-tailed bats like the ones Barbara kept, which means she would probably be able to answer Barbara's questions. (Guide students to include details from the report to support their answer.)

4. Be sure that students identify the report's main ideas and include significant details. Spelling, punctuation, capitalization, and grammar should be correct.

page 64

1. The writer introduced the topic of the report, bats, in the first paragraph.

2. The writer lists all of the sounds that Barbara's bats usually make (chirps, buzzes, and squeals). Then the writer tells us that Barbara had never heard this song before.

3. The fifth paragraph explains how the bats usually act and tells the reader that Hank was different. In the next paragraph, the writer gives specific examples of how Hank's behavior was different from that of the other bats.

4. The first paragraph tells the reader that Barbara would make a scientific discovery. In the last paragraph, the writer explains that the behaviors Barbara observed helped scientists learn more about the bats' mating behaviors.

page 71

1. Daniella is writing to her brother to convince him to come home for Thanksgiving. (Guide students in identifying Daniella's purpose for writing.)

2. Everyone in the family will be there. Abuelito is getting old. It has been a while since Daniella and Carlos have talked. There won't be enough players for the traditional family football game if Carlos doesn't come home. Carlos's friend Marcie is coming home for Thanksgiving. Thanksgiving won't be the same without Carlos. Daniella is making his favorite dessert. (Encourage students to use their own words as they list Daniella's reasons.)

3. It sounds as if Marcie is a good friend, maybe even someone Carlos thinks is special. (Look for a logical conclusion based on the details in the letter.)

4. Guide students in summarizing the reasons Daniella gives Carlos for coming home. Summaries should be organized in a thoughtful way, with the main ideas and important details clearly presented.

page 72

1. "I just wish you were going to be here to share it with us."

2. I think that Daniella is trying to make her brother feel guilty for not coming home. She suggests that her grandfather might not live much longer and that Carlos is his favorite grandson.

3. I think Carlos will feel guilty about choosing to visit his roommate's family for Thanksgiving instead of going home. Daniella's letter is packed with examples of why it is important to her and her family to have Carlos home over the holidays. These examples will make him picture everyone at home and remember all the fun they've had in past years.

4. I think that Daniella was planting the idea that Carlos's roommate could come home with him, rather than the other way around.

page 79

1. The Ogre is not your usual hero. He isn't handsome and he prefers to live alone. (Encourage students to paraphrase the details.)

2. Other important characters in the movie are Princess Stella, the moles, and Manco, the villain.

3. Bernie rescues the princess from a dragon so the moles will go back to their village and leave Bernie alone in the forest. (Guide students to include the major events from the review.)

4. Check to see that students identify the purpose of the review and summarize its significant points. Summaries should be organized in a thoughtful way, with the main reasons for seeing the movie and the important details clearly presented.

page 80

1. The writer outlines the elements of a fairy tale, which are familiar to everyone. Then the writer tells the reader that the characters in this fairy tale are different, making this the funniest fairy tale ever.

2. The writer doesn't want to spoil the movie for the reader, but he or she wants to share a few exciting moments to convince the reader to see the movie.

3. Most movies have people or look like cartoons. It is so amazing for a computer-animated movie to look this realistic that people will want to see it.

4. In the first paragraph, the writer presents the opinion that *Bernie, the Laughing Ogre* is one of the funniest fairy tales ever. In the last paragraph, the writer restates the opinion and summarizes the reasons the reader should see the movie.

page 87

1. After the Mexican-American War ended, Mexico owed money to France. France was unwilling to accept late payments, so Napoleon III sent troops to Mexico to take over the country. (Help students paraphrase the information for their answers.)

2. The French forces had better equipment and training. They also had more soldiers. In addition, the French had not lost one battle in 50 years. (Guide students to include all significant details.)

3. The Mexican army at Puebla was made up of both soldiers and members of the community. The citizens fought using farm tools as their weapons. (Look for logical conclusions supported by details from the essay.)

4. Check to see that students identify the purpose of the essay and summarize its significant points. Summaries should be organized in a thoughtful way, with the main reasons for celebrating Cinco de Mayo and the important details clearly presented.

page 88

1. "It is a Mexican holiday that all Americans should observe."

2. The movement of the French toward Mexico City forced the Mexican president to flee to northern Mexico. This prevented Confederate forces from receiving supplies from the French army. Without these supplies, Confederate troops were not strong enough to defeat the Union forces.

3. The last two paragraphs summarize the reasons that Americans should celebrate Cinco de Mayo.

4. The first paragraph gives the reader information about Cinco de Mayo and states the writer's opinion. The last paragraphs list reasons that support the writer's opinion and that try to convince the reader to agree with the writer.